CHEROKEE DESCENDANTS EAST

AN INDEX TO THE GUION MILLER APPLICATIONS

VOLUME I

Cherokee Potter Maude French Welch and her granddaughter "Koodaloo" Joyce Welch Tranter

TRANSCRIBED BY
JEFF BOWEN
NATIVE STUDY
Gallipolis, Ohio
USA

Copyright © 2011
by Jeff Bowen

ALL RIGHTS RESERVED
No part of this publication may be reproduced
or used in any form or manner whatsoever
without previous written permission from the
copyright holder or publisher.

Originally published:
Baltimore, Maryland
2011

Reprinted by:

Native Study LLC
Gallipolis, OH
www.nativestudy.com

Library of Congress Control Number: 2020915858

ISBN: 978-1-64968-035-8

Made in the United States of America.

This book is dedicated to Joyce Welch Tranter (Koo da loo). A very special and dear true-blood Cherokee without whose inspiration and friendship this work would not be so meaningful.

Love you and God bless.

Other Books and Series by Jeff Bowen

1901-1907 Native American Census Seneca, Eastern Shawnee, Miami, Modoc, Ottawa, Peoria, Quapaw, and Wyandotte Indians (Under Seneca School, Indian Territory)

1932 Census of The Standing Rock Sioux Reservation with Births And Deaths 1924-1932

Census of The Blackfeet, Montana, 1897- 1901 Expanded Edition

Eastern Cherokee by Blood, 1906-1910, Volumes I thru XIII

Choctaw of Mississippi Indian Census 1929-1932 with Births and Deaths 1924-1931   Volume I

Choctaw of Mississippi Indian Census 1933, 1934 & 1937, Supplemental Rolls to 1934 & 1935 with Births and Deaths 1932-1938, and Marriages 1936-1938 Volume II

Eastern Cherokee Census Cherokee, North Carolina 1930-1939 Census 1930-1931 with Births And Deaths 1924-1931 Taken By Agent L. W. Page Volume I

Eastern Cherokee Census Cherokee, North Carolina 1930-1939 Census 1932-1933 with Births And Deaths 1930-1932 Taken By Agent R. L. Spalsbury   Volume II

Eastern Cherokee Census Cherokee, North Carolina 1930-1939 Census 1934-1937 with Births and Deaths 1925-1938 and Marriages 1936 & 1938 Taken by Agents R. L. Spalsbury And Harold W. Foght Volume III

Seminole of Florida Indian Census, 1930-1940 with Birth and Death Records, 1930-1938

Texas Cherokees 1820-1839 A Document For Litigation 1921

Choctaw By Blood Enrollment Cards 1898-1914 Volumes I thru XVII

Starr Roll 1894 (Cherokee Payment Rolls) Districts: Canadian, Cooweescoowee, and Delaware Volume One

Starr Roll 1894 (Cherokee Payment Rolls) Districts: Flint, Going Snake, and Illinois   Volume Two

Starr Roll 1894 (Cherokee Payment Rolls) Districts: Saline, Sequoyah, and Tahlequah; Including Orphan Roll Volume Three

Other Books and Series by Jeff Bowen

Cherokee Intruder Cases Dockets of Hearings 1901-1909 Volumes I & II

Indian Wills, 1911-1921 Records of the Bureau of Indian Affairs
Books One thru Seven;

Native American Wills & Probate Records 1911-1921

Turtle Mountain Reservation Chippewa Indians 1932 Census with Births & Deaths, 1924-1932

Chickasaw By Blood Enrollment Cards 1898-1914 Volume I thru V

Visit our website at **www.nativestudy.com** to learn more about these and other books and series by Jeff Bowen

NATIONAL ARCHIVES MICROFILM PUBLICATIONS

INTRODUCTION

On the 348 rolls of this microfilm publication are reproduced the applications submitted for shares of the money that was appropriated for the Eastern Cherokee Indians by the Congress on June 30, 1906. The Eastern Cherokee applications, August 29, 1906 - May 26, 1909, are part of the Guion Miller Enrollment Records that are among the records of the U.S. Court of Claims. This publication also includes a general index to Eastern Cherokee applications (two vols.).

History

Before the U.S. Court of Claims was established in 1855 there was no procedure by which claims arising against the U.S. Government could be enforced by suit. Consideration of claims was provided for when the Treasury Department was established in 1789; later acts of the Congress authorized the Department to settle all claims by or against the Government. If a claim was rejected by the Treasury Department, the claimant's only course of action was to appeal directly to the Congress. Petitions to that body for relief had become so numerous by the middle of the 19th century that the Congress was beginning to find it impossible to make the proper and necessary investigations for actions on the claims.

The U.S. Court of Claims was established by an act of February 24, 1855, to hear claims against the United States including those referred to the court by the Congress, based on any law of the Congress, any regulation of an executive department, or any contract with the Government, whether explicit or implied. Under this act the court served only as a fact finding agency, and its conclusions were submitted to the Congress for approval and for the granting of awards. In 1863 the Congress enlarged the court's jurisdiction and gave it authority to render judgments against the Government, with the right of appeal to the Supreme Court. An act of 1925 abolished appeals from the Court of Claims to the Supreme Court and substituted writs of certiorari.

An act approved July 1, 1902 (32 Stat. 726), gave the Court of Claims jurisdiction over any claim arising under treaty stipulations that the Cherokee Tribe, or any band thereof, might have against the United States and over any claims that the United States might have against any Cherokee Tribe or band. Suit for such a claim was to be instituted within 2 years after the act was approved. As a result, three suits were brought before the court concerning grievances arising out of the treaties:

NATIONAL ARCHIVES MICROFILM PUBLICATIONS

(1) *The Cherokee Nation* v. *The United States*, General-Jurisdiction Case No. 23199; (2) *The Eastern and Emigrant Cherokees* v. *The United States*, General-Jurisdiction Case No. 23212; and (3) *The Eastern Cherokees* v. *The United States*, General-Jurisdiction Case No. 23214.

On May 18, 1905, the court decided in favor of the Eastern Cherokees and instructed the Secretary of the Interior to identify the persons entitled to participate in the distribution of funds for payment of the claims. On June 30, 1906, the Congress appropriated more than $1 million for this purpose. The task of compiling a roll of eligible persons was begun by Guion Miller, special agent of the Interior Department. In a decree of April 29, 1908, the court (1) vacated that part of its earlier decision that had given the Secretary of the Interior responsibility for determing[sic] the eligbility[sic] of claimants and (2) appointed Miller as a special commissioner of the Court of Claims.

The same decree also provided that the fund was to be distributed to all Eastern and Western Cherokee Indians who were alive on May 28, 1906, who could establish the fact that at the time of the treaties they were members of the Eastern Cherokee Tribe or were descendants of such persons, and that they had not been affiliated with any tribe of Indians other than the Eastern Cherokee or the Cherokee Nation. The decree further provided that claimants should already have applications on file with the Commissioner of Indian Affairs, or should file such applications with the special commissioner of the Court of Claims on or before August 31, 1907. Additionally, applications for minors and persons of unsound mind were to be filed by their parents or persons having their care and custody, and applications for persons who had died after May 28, 1906, were to be filed by their children or legal representatives.

In his report of May 28, 1909, Miller stated that 45,847 separate applications had been filed, representing a total of about 90,000 individual claimants, 30,254 of whom were enrolled as entitled to share in the fund – 3,203 residing east and 27,051 residing west of the Mississippi River. On June 10, 1909, the court confirmed and approved the roll, submitted by Miller in his report, of Eastern Cherokees who were entitled to a share of the fund except "so much as shall be expected [excepted] to on or before August 30, 1909." After the exceptions had been filed and investigated, Miller submitted a supplemental report and roll to the court on January 5, 1910. In this report he stated that about 11,750 exceptions had been made, that the names of 610 persons [238 east and 372 west if the Mississippi] had been added to the roll, and that the names of 44 persons [5 east and 39 west of the Mississippi] had be stricken from the roll because clerical errors in enrollment had been discovered. Thus the final figure on the total number of persons entitled to share in the fund was 30, 820, of which 3,436 persons resided east and 27,384 resided west of the Mississippi River. On March 15, 1910, the court finally decreed that the rolls be approved and that, after certain deductions for expenditures, payments were to be made equally among the Eastern Cherokees who enrolled. The court also authorized the Secretary of the Treasury to issue a warrant in favor of each person.

In certifying the eligibility of the Cherokees, Miller used earlier census lists and rolls that had been made of the Cherokees by Hester, Chapman, Drennen and others between 1835 and 1884. Copies of some of these rolls and the indexes to them are filed with the Miller records [filmed as M685]. Other enrollment records used by Miller are among the classified subject files of the Bureau and are designated as "33931-11-053 Cherokee Nation."

Records

The applications contain sworn evidences of identity and were filed with the Interior Department's Office of Indian Affairs until April 29, 1907 [the last application was No. 22268], after which the applications were filed directly with the court. The application required each claimant to state fully his or her English and Indian names, residence, age, place of birth, name of husband or wife, name of tribe, and names of children. It further required the English and Indian names of the claimant's parents and grandparents, place of their birth, place of their residence in 1851 if they were living at that time, dates of their death, and a statement as to whether any of them had ever before been enrolled as Indians for annuities or other benefits and, if so, with what tribe. Each claimant was also to furnish the names of all brothers and sisters, with their ages and residences, and the names and residences of all uncles and aunts. Applications were required to be made under oath and to be supported by affidavits of two witnesses who were well acquainted with the applicant. With each application is a card showing final action taken and the reasons therefore. Filed with many of the applications are inquiries concerning the status of the cases, requests for further evidence, protests about unfavorable actions, form letters that had been sent by the special commissioner to the applicants as notices of rejection of their applications and returned by the Post Office Department as unclaimed, affidavits and statements of witnesses, powers of attorney, and last wills and testaments. The applications are arranged by the number assigned at the time the application was received. There are some gaps in the application numbers; these are explained on insert sheets at the appropriate places on the film. The index is arranged alphabetically by name [either English or Indian] of claimant.

NATIONAL ARCHIVES MICROFILM PUBLICATIONS

Many of the files contain a cross-reference card to other applications. This cross-reference card often refers to the EX file, the report on exceptions filed by Miller on January 5, 1910.

Related Records

The records reproduced in this microfilm publication are part of the records in the custody of the National Archives and Records Service [NARS] designated as Records of the U.S. Court of Claims, Record Group [RG] 123. Among related records in this record group are additional records relating to Miller's enrollment of the Eastern Cherokees. These include receipts for Treasury warrants and miscellaneous correspondence, 1906 - 11. The original of these records is in RG 123; a copy is in RG 75.

Some related records in Records of the Bureau of Indian Affairs, RG 75, have been reproduced as NARS Microfilm Publication T496, *Census Roll, 1835, of the Cherokee Indians East of the Mississippi and Index to the Roll.* Also in RG 75 are the classified subject files of the Bureau.

Records Relating to Enrollment of Eastern Cherokees by Guion Miller, 1908-10, M685, contains the general index to Eastern Cherokee applications, 2 volumes; the report submitted by Guion Miller, May 28, 1909, 10 volumes; the roll of Eastern Cherokees, May 28, 1909; the report on exceptions filed, January 5, 1910; the supplemental roll of Eastern Cherokees, January 5, 1910; transcripts of testimony, February, 1908 - March, 1909, 10 volumes; various indexes and rolls of Eastern Cherokee Indians, 1851, 1854, and 1884; and miscellaneous notes and drafts.

Additional records relating to the enrollment of Eastern Cherokee Indians are in Records of the Office of the Secretary of the Interior, Record Group 48.

These records were prepared for filming by Jestine Turner and William D. Grover, who also prepared these introductory remarks.

THE EASTERN CHEROKEES

v.   No. 23,214

THE UNITED STATES

ORDER.

Ordered this 10th day of June, 1909, that the report of Special Commissioner Guion Miller, bearing date the 28th day of May, 1909, together with the exhibits therewith, including the roll of the individual Eastern Cherokees reported by the said Special Commissioner as entitled to participate in the fund arising from Item 2 of the judgment filed in this cause, be received and filed in this cause.

2. It is further ordered that the said Special Commissioner cause the said roll of individual Eastern Cherokees found by him to be entitled to share in said fund, to be printed and distributed.

3. It is further ordered hat the said roll of individual Eastern Cherokees entitled to share in the fund arising from the judgment in this cause, as reported by Special Commissioner Guion Miller on the 28th day of May, 1909, be and the same is hereby approved, ratified and confirmed, except as to so much of the same as shall be specially excepted to on or before the 30th day of August, 1909. All such exceptions shall be forwarded to the Clerk of the Court of Claims, Washington, D.C., and shall be in writing, and shall state fully the grounds upon which such exceptions are based, and shall be supported by an affidavit of a person having knowledge of the facts and shall contain the name, age and post office address of each individual claimed

to have been omitted from said roll, or to have been improperly placed thereon. Said exceptions and affidavits shall be filed in duplicate in each case, but only the originals must be sworn to. In case an exception is filed on behalf of an individual whose name has been omitted from said roll the said exception shall set forth fully the English and Indian name, the ancestor through whom claim is made, who was living in 1835 or 1851, and shall give the age of said ancestor in 1835 or 1851. Such exceptions must further state the number of the claimant's application. All such exceptions shall be set down for hearing on the third Monday in October, 1909.

Sample Application

The following information obtained from Microfilm M1104- Roll # *129*, Cherokee (Eastern & Western) Applications of the U.S. Court of Claims.

Application No. *12996*	**Action:** *Admitted*
Name: *Awee S. French* and *5* children.	
Residence: *Birdtown, NC*	
Reasons: *The mother of applicant was enrolled as Sic - ow - ih, by Chapman in 1851, 423. Father probably enrolled by Chapman as Sal - lah - lih, or Squirrel; 240.*	

Commissioner of Indian Affairs,   Washington, D.C.

Sir:

    I hereby make application for such share as may be due me of the fund appropriated by the Act of Congress, approved June 30, 1906, in accordance with the Decrees of the Court of Claims of May 18, 1905, and May 28, 1906, in favor of the Eastern Cherokees. The evidence of identity is herewith subjoined.

1. State full name:
   - English name: *Awee S. French*
   - Indian name: *do*

2. Residence: *Birdtown*

3. Town and post office: *Birdtown*

4. County: *Swain*   5. State: *North Carolina*

Sample Application

6. Date and place of birth: *1877   Graham Co, NC*

7. By what right do you claim to share? If you claim through more than one relative living in 1851, set forth each claim separately:
Father, Solole or Squirrel; Father's father Oo - cl ? ? ? - no -tah; Father's mother, Quar lar you yar; Father's brothers & mothers viz: Oo - clun - nor - tal, Squirrel deceased - or Little Squirrel deceased; one aunt, Dorky Fox. Or Dor - kie

8. Are you married?   *yes*

9. Name and age of wife or husband: *W.L. French   age 40 yrs.*

10. Give names of your father and mother, and your mother's name before marriage:

Father - English name: *Squirrel*

Indian name: *Solole*

Mother - English name: *Sallie Wilnote*

Indian name: *Se - gar - wee*

Maiden name: *Se - gar - wee Lorch*

11. Where were they born?

Father: *Graham Co, NC*

Mother: *Soco Creek, near Qualla, Jackson Co, NC*

Sample Application

12. Where did they reside in 1851, if living at that time

Father: _Graham Co, NC_   Mother: _Graham Co, NC_

13. Date of death of your father and mother:

Father: _8-1895_   Mother: _living_

14. Were they ever enrolled for annuities, land or other benefits? If so, state when and where:
Father in 1835, place unknown, and 1847 and 1851, in Graham Co, NC

15. Name all your brothers and sisters, giving ages, and if not living, the date of death:

1) _Sequitch Squirrel   b: ?   In Indian Territory, if living_

2) _Oo - lun - na - nar   b: 1849   d: ?_

3) _Baby Squirrel   dead 1868_

4) _Polly S. Owl   dead 1905_

5) _George Squirrel   b: 1866   living_

6) _Noah Squirrel   dead 1891_

7) _David Squirrel   b: 1874   living_

8) _Dah - nie   b: 1886   d: 1899_

Sample Application

16. State English and Indian names of your grandparents on both father's and mother's side, if possible:

Father's side: **Wilnote**   **Oo - thin - no - dah**
Guar - lai - you - gar

Mother's side: **mother living**

17. Where were they born? **unknown**

18. Where did they reside in 1851, if living at that time? **unknown**

19. Give names of all their children, and residence, if living, if not living, give dates of death:

1) **George Wilnote   Char - che   Oo - thin - no - dah**
d: 7-17-1893

2) **Dorky Fox   Dah - gih   d: 1870**

3) **Squirrel   Salole   d: 1895**

4) **Dah - nah - ih   same   d: ?**

5) **Aggie   A - kee   d: 10-27-1865**

20. Have you ever been enrolled for annuities, land or other benefits? If so, state when and where

1883 by J.G. Nester

Sample Application

21. To expedite identification, claimants should given the full English and Indians names, if possible, of their paternal and maternal ancestors back to 1835:

Oo - thin - no - dah	&	*Yoh - na - gus - kei*
Grandfather	&	*Great Grandfather*

REMARKS
(Under this head the applicant may give any additional information that he believes will assist in proving his claim.)

I solemnly swear that the foregoing statements made by me re true to the best of my knowledge and belief.

(Signature) *Awee S. French*

Subscribed and sworn to before me this 17th day of *January*

5-9-1910

Received of Guion Miller, Special Commissioner of the Court of Claims, Treasury Warrant No. 9790, 9791, 9792, 9793, 9794, 9795 each for the sum of $133.19 in full settlement of amount due the beneficiary or beneficiaries enrolled opposite Roll # 842 - 3 - 4 - 5 - 6 - 7 on the Final Roll of the Eastern Cherokees entitled to share in the fund arising from the judgment of the Court of Claims of May 28, 1906, as approved by said Court, March 15, 1910.

Signed by   Awee S. French

Sample Application

Supplemental Application for Minor Children

Special Commissioner of the Court of Claims,
601 Ouray Building, Washington, D.C.

Sir:
    I hereby make application for such share as may be due my minor children of the fund appropriated by the Act of Congress approved June 30, 1906, in accordance with the decree of the Court of Claims of May 18, 1905, and May 28, 1906, in favor of the Eastern Cherokees, and I ask that this be made part of my original application, No. *12996*.

1. State your full name: *Awee S. French*

2. Residence and post office: *Birdtown & Birdtown*

3. County: *Swain*   4. State: *NC*

5. Date and place of birth: *1878*   *Graham Co, NC*

6. Are you married?   *yes*

7. Name and age of wife or husband: *Wm. L. French   41 yrs*

8. To what tribe of Indians, if any, does he or she belong?
Cherokee Tribe West [Cherokee Nation]

9. Name (age and date of birth) of all your children who were living on May 28, 1906:

1) *Maud French   13   (b) 5-25-1894*

2) *Maronie French 10   (b) 12-15-1897*

Sample Application

3) *Morgan French 8 (b) 12-23-1899*

4) *Soggie French 6 (b) 3-23-1901*

5) *George B French 3 (b) 5-21-1904*

10. Were they ever enrolled for money, annuities, land or other benefits? If so, state when and where, and with what tribe of Indians: *no*

REMARKS
(Under this head the applicant may give any additional facts which will assist in proving his claim.)

Grandfather, Sololi or Squirrel, on roll of 1835-36, 1846 & 1851 with Eastern Cherokee Indians - One child born since, May 28, 1906, Jonah French, born 3-12-1907

I solemnly swear that the foregoing statements made by me are true to the best of my knowledge and belief.

[Signature]   *Awee S. French*

Subscribed and sworn to before me this   *14* day of *June* , 1907.

INTRODUCTION

Between May, 1905, and April, 1907, the U.S. Supreme Court authorized the Secretary of the Interior to identify the descendants of Eastern Cherokees entitled to participate in the distribution of more than $1 million in outstanding claims against the U.S. government based upon the Treaties of 1835-36 and 1845. On May 28, 1909, Commissioner Guion Miller, representing the Interior Department, submitted to Congress his findings with respect to 45,857 separate applications for compensation (totaling about 90,000 individual Native American claimants). Miller qualified about 30,000 persons inhabiting approx. 39 states and 3 countries to share in the fund. Ninety percent of the eligible were living west of the Mississippi River.

Among the records created by the Guion Miller Commission are (1) an Index to the 45,000 Eastern and Western Cherokee Applications (National Archives Record Group 123) and (2) a collection of Abstracts of the Commission's findings, arranged by application number (Record Group M685). The Index—the subject of this series—and the Abstracts contain complimentary information and together provide a detailed accounting of the Cherokee applicants and their family members.

The work at hand, *Cherokee Descendants East: An Index to the Guion Miller Applications*, is a verbatim transcription of the first portion of the index found on National Archives Record Group 123. It refers to the Cherokee applicants living East of the Mississippi River in 1909 (about 3,200 applicants, or 10% of the total). For each head of household named in the application we are given the following additional information: Guion Miller roll number, city and state of residence, and the names of other householders with their ages and relationship to the head. A history of the Guion Miller Commission and several sample applications precede the index of applicants, while an addendum and comprehensive name index conclude the work. Two additional, larger volumes will cover Cherokee applicants residing West of the Mississippi.

As alluded to above, persons interested in Cherokee genealogy should also consult the Abstracts of the Guion Miller Commission applications. This information has been published in the 12-volume series, *Eastern Cherokee by Blood, 1906-1910*, by this author. These abstracts name the applicant, the number of persons in the household, an abstract of each enrollee's case, and the disposition (admitted or rejected), including cross-references to other applications and connections to other families.

NB The contents of this book was originally published in 1996.

Jeff Bowen
Gallipolis, Ohio
www.NativesStudy.com

Roll
of
Eastern Cherokees

**ENTITLED TO PARTICIPATE IN THE FUND
ARISING FROM THE JUDGMENT OF THE
COURT OF CLAIMS OF MAY 28, 1906**

AS REPORTED BY

GUION MILLER, SPECIAL COMMISSIONER

May twenty-eight, nineteen hundred and nine

EASTERN CHEROKEES RESIDING EAST OF MISSISSIPPI RIVER.

KEY: Guion Miller Application Number; Name; Address; Relation (to Head); Age in 1906

28115 ADAMS, Adaline, Andrews, NC, 23; Gudger, S, 5; Lewie, S, 2
16416 ADAMS, Ina, New York City, NY, 156-8 Broadway, 25
22832 ADAMS, Rolling, Marble, NC, 22; Nora, D, 4; Monell, S, 2
 1815 ADAMS, Vinia, Marble, NC, 45; Ethel E, D, 15;   John V, S, 13
22834 ADAMS, Walter, Marble, NC, 24; Willard, S, 5; Harry, S, 2; Frank S, 1/6
15865 AH-HIH-DAH, Birdtown, NC, 50; [Alexander, Geo M See #12141] [Alexander, Jeanie M See #12141]
23882 ALLEN, John, Birdtown, NC, 35; **15840,** Eve, W, 30; Emmerline, D, 6
15705 ALLEN, Will, Birdtown, NC, 52; **15707,** Sallie, W, 50; Junn-lus-kie, S, 17; Rebecca, GD, 10
26831 ALLISON, Nannie, Cherokee, NC, 23; Roy Robert, S, 3; Albert Monroe, S, 2
31243 ALTON, Burduir, Sequatchie, TN, 21
31242 ALTON, Texas, Sequatchie, TN, 47; James, S, 19; John, S, 18; Kate, D, 15; Liney, D, 12; McKinley, S, 9; Claude, S, 6
 1444 ANDERSON, Jane, Culberson, NC, 26; Bessie R, D, 3; Cora O, D, 3
  555 ANDERSON, Rannie, Hill City, TN, 53; Bertha, D, 15; Lillie May, D, 13; Cora Neal, D, 10; Eddie W, S, 9; Beulah, D, 2; Eulah, D, 2; Wilber E, S, 5/12
15791 ARCH, David, Cherokee, NC, 40; **15784,** Martha, W, 20; Ollivan, S, 13; Ross, S, 10
16294 ARCH, Jennie, Cherokee, NC, 67
 6218 ARCH, Johnson, Cherokee, NC, 22
 6658 ARMACHAIN, Conseen, Wahhiyah, NC, 51; **16293,** Susie, W, 47; Ollie, D, 7 [Died 9-25-1906]
 6655 ARMACHAIN, Davis, Wahhiyah, NC, 55; **44458,** Annie, W, 36; Jesse, S, 9; Lewel, D, 7; Rachel, D, 4; 6655, Kahida, D, 1 5; Severe, S, ½
33889 ARMACHAIN, Lacy, Cherokee, NC, 29; **33888,** Anna, W, 32
 6656 ARMACHAIN, Severe, Wahhiyah, NC, 63; **16287,** Anna Eliza, W, 47; Jonie, S, 12

[ARNEACH, Anna See #6765] *(Note: entry separate from other family groups)*

10804 ARNEACH, Jefferson, Almond, NC, 32; **15780,** Sarah, W, 31; Bird, David, S, 13; Lizzie, D, 10; Bessie, D, 6
10063 ARNEACH, Jenny, Cherokee, NC, 74

[ARNEACH, Mary See #10064] *(Note: entry separate from other family groups)*

10065 ARNEACH, Will W, Cherokee, NC, 57; James K, S, 13; Nell, D, 10; Buck, S, 7
25906 ARNOLD, Jess, Calhoun, TN, 33; Beckie, D, 14; Allie, D, 13; Ruby, D, 8; Lula, D, 6; Dock, S, 3
25907 ARNOLD, John, Calhoun, TN, 47; Prince, S, 18; Arthur, S, 16; Martha, D, 12; DO, D, 7; Henry, S, 5
37315 ASAY, Sarah Diannah, Vincentown, NJ, 27
10447 ASHMAN, Laura, Chicago, IL, 52; 116 North Clark St
22633 ATKINS, Emmet D, Russellville, KY, 28; James M, S, 1/12
27413 ATKINS, James Wm, Gastonia, NC, 26

EASTERN CHEROKEES RESIDING EAST OF MISSISSIPPI RIVER.

KEY: Guion Miller Application Number; Name; Address; Relation (to Head); Age in 1906

22634 ATKINS, Mary F, Russellville, KY, 24
  875 ATKINS, Ruth D, Russellville, KY, 48; Lillian J, D, 20; Bennie Weaver, S, 18
 3762 AUSTIN, Nana, Chattanooga, TN, 36; 117 Lewis St; James, S, 16; Maggie, D, 11; Jackson, S, 6; Lelah, D, 9; Alice, D, 3
16022 AXE, David, Cherokee, NC, 63
 8402 AXE, Jennie, Tomotla, NC, 52
  729 AXE, John D, Robbinsville, NC, 56; 731, Eva, W, 45
16834 AXE, Josiah, Cherokee, NC, 39; Amos, S, 4; Nancy, D, 3; Eighty, S, 1

[AXE, Lucinda See #24443]
[AXE, Peter See #24443] *(Note: entries separate from other family groups)*
[AXE, Mandy See #24443]

[AXE, Sam Smoker See #16832] *(Note: entry separate from other family groups)*

 8641 AXE, Willie, Robbinsville, NC, 29; 8642, Caroline, W, 35; Maggie, D, 11; Sarah, D, 5

43117 BAGWELL, Joseph A, Rome, GA, 24; 303 6th Avenue
 2631 BAGWELL, Kate, Rome, GA, 44; 101 8th Avenue; Hoydt, S, 18; [McDONALD, Mary See #4175]; Bagwell, Francis E, D, 14; Carl, S, 11; Pearl, D, 11; Susie, D, 10; Carrie, D, 6; Florence, D, 3; John Berry, S, 1
  797 BAKER, Elizabeth, Sweet Gun, GA, 48; Arthur, S, 15
27221 BAKER, Ellen M, Bryson City, NC, 28; Stella, D, 8; Charley, S, 3; Mary, D, 1
  798 BAKER, Elmira, Sweet Gun, GA, 37; Luther, S, 14; Mary A or Dona, D, 12; Worldly, S, 9; Cricket, D, 5
35453 BARKSDALE, Belle, Cressville, AL, 19; RR #2; Jewry, S, 2; Mabel, D, 1/12
 6395 BARNS, Mary, Gallaway, GA, 25; Barney, S, 5; Galley, ?, 1
45297 BARNWELL, Elizabeth, Shellyville, KY, 49; Carleton, S, 18
45298 BARNWELL, Middleton S, Shellyville, KY, 24
45299 BARNWELL, Stephen E, Takoma Park, DC, 28
 7564 BARRETT, Mary Alice, Cumming, GA, 23; Clara J, D, 3
  915 BATTLE, Adaline E, Andrews, NC, 54; Addie E, D, 19; Zed P, S, 17
23415 BATTLE, Bruce W, Andrews, NC, 25
31216 BATTLE, Laura E, Andrews, NC, 21
31215 BATTLE, Lox V, Andrews, NC, 21
31213 BATTLE, William M, Andrews, NC, 23
16028 BAUER, Fred B, Cherokee, NC, 10; By Josephine Blythe, Gdn
11214 BAUER, Owenah A, Bellaire, OH, 11; By John A Schick, Gdn
16333 BEAN, Ollie, Birdtown, NC, 26
15712 BEARMEAT, Mary, Birdtown, NC, 60
33447 BECK, Berry B, Clayton, GA, 26
31170 BECK, Emory S, Clayton, GA, 27
  808 BECK, James, Clayton, GA, 55; Nancy S, D, 20; Noah, S, 10
31168 BECK, Lillie F, Clayton, GA, 29; Fletcher, S, 13
  807 BECK, Mary A, Clayton, GA, 28; Edith D, D, 3

EASTERN CHEROKEES RESIDING EAST OF MISSISSIPPI RIVER.

KEY: Guion Miller Application Number; Name; Address; Relation (to Head); Age in 1906

   760 BECK, Samuel, Clayton, GA, 49; 31167, Eugene W, S, 19; Samuel, Jr, S, 17; Rose, D, 15; Thomas, S, 13; May D, 10; Major J, S, 7
   758 BECK, Sarah, Clayton, GA, 54
31169 BECK, Savannah G, Clayton, GA, 22
 4118 BELL, Albert M, Sheltonville, GA, 48; John, S, 16; Anice, D, 12; Harley E, S, 10; Lucile, D, 8; Rubey, D, 5
  933 BELL, Edward E, Milledgeville, GA, 26
10455 BELL, Eleanor B, St Elmo, TN, 18; By Ada Jane Bell, Gdn
 4120 BELL, George A, Sheltonville, GA, 30
10460 BELL, Henry Charlton, St Elmo, TN, 20; By Ada Jane Bell, Gdn
10459 BELL, Isla May, St Elmo, TN, 25
 4119 BELL, Mary Jane, Sheltonville, GA, 51
 4123 BELL, Mary McNair, Sheltonville GA,10; By Walter L Bell, Gdn
10457 BELL, Raymond B, St Elmo, TN, 23
 4125 BELL, Reuben E, Sheltonville, GA, 13; By Walter L Bell, Gdn
 4121 BELL, Virgil E, Sheltonville, GA, 16; By Walter L Bell, Gdn
 4122 BELL, Walter L, Sheltonville, GA, 42; Basil R, S, 1/12
 4117 BELL, Wilber P, Shelton, GA, 36
10456 BELL, Willard, St Elmo, TN, 12; By Ada Jane Bell, Gdn
 4124 BELL, William A Sheltonville, GA, 5; By Walter L Bell, Gdn
15697 BEN, Cheech, Birdtown, NC, 28; Stand, S, 4; Ollie, D, 2
18855 BENGE, Hooley, Augusta, GA, 32; May, D, 6; Samson, S, 4; Mitchell, S, 2; Richard, S, 2
26177 BENNETT, Alice, Plainsville, GA, 27
 3231 BENSON, Alonzo M, Dahlonega, GA, 30; Horner H, S, 8; Moye, D, 3; Leslie, S, 1
 3233 BENSON, Rebecca M, Dahlonega, GA, 51; Ezekiel, S, 6
 7569 BETTIS, Harriet Anna, Cumming, GA, 47; RFD #1
 7566 BETTIS, Nellie Jim, Cumming, GA, 14; RFD #1
 7567 BETTIS, Robert Knox, Dalton, GA, 25; Ralph K, S, 4; James H, S, 2
 7568 BETTIS, Roy Henry, Cumming, GA, 18; RFD #1
 7565 BETTIS, Virgil, Cumming, GA, 21
35237 BIDDIX, Rosa, Cherokee, NC, 27; Mary Jane, D, 3

[EUBANKS, Martha L See #34072] *(Note: entry separate from other family groups)*

15789 BIGMEAT, Auneka, Cherokee, NC, 44; Adam, S, 19
15775 BIGMEAT, Isaiah, Cherokee, NC, 39; 15793, Sarah, W, 26
 8595 BIGMEAT, Nickademas, Andrews, NC, 30; 8594, Nancy, W, 46
15860 BIGMEAT, Robert, Cherokee, NC, 17, Minda, Sis, 10; By Rachel Reed, Gdn
16790 BIGMEAT, Yona, Cherokee, NC, 35
 7751 BIGWITCH, Charlie, Cherokee, NC, 20
16030 BIGWITCH, Joseph, Cherokee, NC, 35; 15325, Sallie Long, W, 29; Lucy, D, 1; Alice, D, 8
11118 BIRD, Bird C, Cherokee, NC, 36; 11115, Ollie, W, 33; Nan, D, 16; Colinda, D, 16; Dan, S, 8

EASTERN CHEROKEES RESIDING EAST OF MISSISSIPPI RIVER.

KEY: Guion Miller Application Number; Name; Address; Relation (to Head); Age in 1906

42913 BIRD, Dan, Tomotla, NC, 27; 16262, Polly, W, 24; Bettie, D, 6; Solomon, S, 4

[BIRD, David See #15780]
[BIRD, Lizzie See #15780]   *(Note: entries separate from other family groups)*
[BIRD, Bessie See #15780]

29369 BIRD, Loyd, Birdtown, NC, 26; 29397, Ollie, W, 27; Annie, D, 1/40; Wildcat, Lestie, D of W, 10
6629 BIRD, Spencer, Cherokee, NC, 60; 6631, Lize, W, 67
16295 BIRD, Steve, Tomotla, NC, 57; 10022, Annie, W, 51
10020 BIRD, Timpson, Cherokee, NC, 22
15825 BIRD, Tohiskie, Big Cove, NC, 64; 11107, Bird, Sill, W, 57; Quattie, D, 16
12752 BIRD, Going, Wahhayah, NC, 40; 12755, Wallie, W, 43; Bettie, D, 10; Eli, S, 13
2361 BLACK, Mary E, McCays, TN, 29; Arthur C, S, 12; William E, S, 11; Roy R, S, 7; John H, S, 3
14741 BLACKFOX, Charles, Cherokee, NC, 25; Lloyd, S, 3
16793 BLACKFOX, Cindy, Cherokee, NC, 57
7748 BLACKFOX, Josiah, Wahhiyah, NC, 57; 15822, Diahnah, W, 51; Joe, S, 11
15755 BLANKENSHIP Rebecca A, Tailscreek, OK, 60
7731 BLYTHE, Adelia, Cherokee, NC, 42; Jarrett, S, 19
6223 BLYTHE, Arch, Cherokee, NC, 29
16274 BLYTHE, David, Whittier, NC, 44; 11139, Nannie, W, 36; Jackson, Jack, S of W, 13
6210 BLYTHE, Elizabeth, Cherokee, NC, 75
15778 BLYTHE, James, Whittier, NC, 45; RFD (#?)
34193 BLYTHE, Stella, Cherokee, NC, 22
14738 BLYTHE, Will Johnson, Cherokee, NC 36; Riley C, S, 6; Louisia C, D, 2; Lillie J, D, ¼
11116 BLYTHE, William H, Cherokee, NC, 33
13881 BOND, Georgia, Spring Place, GA, 26; Howell, Luther, S, 11; Bond, Willie, S, 7; Elisha, S, 4; Emogene, D, 3; Marvin, S, 1
2772 BOWMAN, Alva R, Chattanooga, TN,31; 20193, Bernice N, D, 1
35451 BRACKETT, Buran, Collinsville, AL, 14; R,R, #4; By Nancy Windsor, Gdn
33666 BRACKETT, Emily J, Blairsville, GA 38
16568 BRACKETT, James B, Tilton, GA, 48; RFD #2; Will, S, 19; Ben, S, 17; Charlies, S, 16; James, S, 14; Richard, S, 12; Olie, D, 10; Earl, S, 3
3841 BRACKETT, James KP, Old Fort, TN, 58; Horace, GS, 15
27761 BRACKETT, Jesse M, Keener, AL, 72; RFD #1
35429 BRACKETT, John, Tilton, GA, 22; Nettie L, D, 4; Ben, S, 2; Jesse, S, 1
3844 BRACKETT, John W, Old Fort TN, 39; Nola, D, 13; James E, S, 10; Carrie, D, 7; Beulah, D, 5
3842 BRACKETT, Martha M, Old Fort, TN, 60
33667 BRACKETT, Merica, Blairsville, GA, 32; Howard, S, 6; Floyd, S, 4; Arvie, ?, 2
35449 BRACKETT, Oscar J, Keener, AK, 25; Jennie, D, 1
33665 BRACKETT, Robert Lee, Blairsville, GA, 40; Fannie, D, 9; Evie, D, 8; Jewel, D, 5; Patrick, S, 3; Junie, D, 1

EASTERN CHEROKEES RESIDING EAST OF MISSISSIPPI RIVER.

KEY: Guion Miller Application Number; Name; Address; Relation (to Head); Age in 1906

2728 BRACKETT, Savilla, Dahlonega GA, 26
3843 BRACKETT, Thomas B, Old Fort, TN 35; Nannie L, D, 7; Lillie D, D, 3; Thomas C, S, 2
33664 BRACKETT, William B, Blairsville, GA, 35; Alvie, D, 11; Ader, D, 9; Clyde, S, 6; Dessie, D, 4; Roy, S, 2
37574 BRACKETT, Willie, Keener, AL, 14; RR #1; Henry, Bro, 11; By Martha Whitten, Gd
16027 BRADLEY, Eliza Jane, Big Cove, NC, 36; James W, S, 12; William Amos, S, 10; Henry TD, S, 6; Judson, W, S, 4; Lidda, D, 1
15808 BRADLEY George, Cherokee, NC, 28; Annie, D, 5; Dinah, D, 4; Maggie, D, 2
15809 BRADLEY, Joseph, Cherokee, NC, 24
12769 BRADLEY, Henry, Cherokee, NC, 23

[BRADLEY, James See #15785] *(Note: entry separate from other family groups)*

12770 BRADLEY, Lizzie, Cherokee, NC, 19
15773 BRADLEY, Minda, Cherokee, NC, 16; Morgan, Bro, 14; Nick, Bro, 11; Sarah, Sis, 5; By Vandalia Bradley, Gdn

[BRADLEY, Nancy See #15785] *(Note: entry separate from other family groups)*

17206 BRADLEY, Nancy, Big Cove, NC, 30; Margaret M, D, 7; Roy, S, 3; Mindy A, D, ¼
20067 BROOKS, Mollie, Charleston, TN, 44
6647 BROWN, Daniel, Cherokee NC, 7; By Jennie Brown, Gdn
37458 BROWN, Elmer, Cuba City, WI, 21
6647 BROWN, Jennie, Cherokee, NC, 67
16843 BROWN, Jonas, Judson, NC, 25
16823 BROWN, Lydia, Judson, NC, 60; 15810, Peter, S, 19
41740 BROWN, Mary C, Tailscreek, OK, 34; Eva, D, 12; Oliver, S, 10; Mark, S, 8; Luke, S, 5; Georgia, D, 3; Pearl, D, 1
29142 BROWN, Mary Ethel, Suwanee, GA, 32; Rogers Dixon, S, 10; Howard Jerome, S, 9; Daniel, A, S, 6; James V, S, 3
2773 BROWN, Ora L, East Chattanooga, TN, 26; Harry L, S, 6; Jessie M, D, 1 4; Katie L, D, 2
3193 BRYANT, Elizabeth H, Culberson, NC, 45
22833 BRYSON, Edna, Marble, NC, 20; Lena, D, 1
24724 BRUCE, Kissie E, Green Brier, TN, 36; Ida, D, 14; Frank, S, 13; Eva, D, 11; Harvey, S, 7; Essie, D, 5
801 BRUCE, Thomas, Culberson, NC, 27
34000 BRUNNETT, Sidie, Blue Ridge, GA, 23; Willie, S, 7; Lela, D, 3
35738 BUNCH, Nancy E, Adairsville, GA, 33; Carrie L, D, 8; Matison, S, 5; Myrtle, D, 3; Morris, S, 1/24
6657 BURGESS, Georgia Sneed, Birdtown, NC, 37; Mary M, D, 13; Bessie L, D, 11; Bob Floy, S, 8; Will Rose, S, 3; George A, S, ½
30967 BURNETT, Martha E, Toney, AL, 31

EASTERN CHEROKEES RESIDING EAST OF MISSISSIPPI RIVER.

KEY: Guion Miller Application Number; Name; Address; Relation (to Head); Age in 1906

15864 BUSHYHEAD, Ben, Birdtown, NC, 20; 15834, Nancy, W, 19

12758 CALHOUN, Morgan, Wahhiyah, NC, 43; 32303, Sallie, W, 44; 12758, Wattie, S, 12; Lloyd, S, 10; Eve, D, 8; Yenkeenee, D, 6; Lawrence, S, 4; Henry, S, 2; Godoquoskie, S, 1
6215 CALLOHOUN, Lawyer, Cherokee, NC, 48; 6196, Ollie, W, 35; Joe, S, 19
11709 CAMP, Jas R, Chattanooga TN, 24
6024 CANOUT, Lizzie, Robbinsville, NC, 65
24441 CANOUT, Maggie, Birdtown, NC, 17
426 CARTER, Martha A, Cherrylog, Ga, 20; Margaret L, D, 4; William H, S, 1
8420 CAT, Johnson, Almond, NC, 49; 8419, Sally, W, 48; 8420, Willie, S, 20; Bettie, D, 17; Margaret, D, 15; Jesse, S, 11; Mandy, D, 8; Lucy, GD, 1
1416 CATE, Elizabeth, Hill City, TN, 65
10076 CATOLST, Charley, Cherokee, NC, 63; 10078, Eve, W, 66
29402 CATOLST, Jim, Cherokee, NC, 25
10075 CATOLST, Nancy, Cherokee, NC, 59
29405 CATOLST, Tamar, Cherokee, NC, 35; 10079, Sallie, W, 20; Eliza Jane, D, 3; Elec, S, 1
29404 CATOLST, Wallace, Cherokee, NC, 30
29403 CATOLST, William, Cherokee, NC, 28
18053 CATT, Sallie, Tomotla, NC, 90
16314 CAYLOR, Nancy E, Calhoun, GA, 37; RFD (#?); Sidney C, S, 15; Mattie E, D, 12; William L, S, 5
4538 CEARLEY, Lucie, Culberson, NC, 27; Luther, S, 6; Emory, S, 4; Robert, S, 2
12120 CHAMBERS, Rosa M, Richmond, VA, 39; 417 W Grace St; William A, Jr, S, 3
13341 CHARLTON, Emily W, Savannah, GA, 30; 4 Henry St West
13345 CHARLTON, Sallie Waters, Savannah, 34; 4 Henry St West
14657 CHARLTON, Wilhelmina H, Savannah, GA, care 461 Oak St, Chattanooga, TN, 45; Catherine H, Savannah, GA, D, 13; Thomas J, S, 11
32188½ CHASTAIN, William B, Chestnut Gap, GA, 10; Wrenie F, Sis, 5; By Mary Chastain, Gdn
26406 CHATMAN, Artie, Plainville, GA, 20
14712 CHATMAN, Martha R, Adairsville, GA, 29; Pendleton, Walter, S, 11; Chatman, Thomas, S, 6; Oscar, S, 1
6199 CHE-WO-NA, Cherokee, NC, 66
24394 CHICKALALA, Andy, Japan, NC, 23
9908 CHICKALEELAH, John, Robbinsville, NC, 100; 10172, Annie, W, 69
26248 CHICKILULA, Stone, Robbinsville, NC, 38; 10173, Mary, W, 37; Jacob, S, 15; Sowanu, D, 9; Loosy, D, 5
10045 CHILDASKI, Will, Cherokee, NC, 56; 10046, Charlotte, p W, 38; Ute Crow, S of W, 19; Queta, D, 3; Waddie, S, 12
10024 CHILDERS, Lula F, Birdtown, NC, 24; Walter, S, 3; Robert, S, 2
10775 CHU-LO-AN-WE, Fidel, Big Cove, NC, 38
15898 CHU-LO-DA-DEGI,Jimmie,Cherokee,NC,50
30178 CHURCH, Mary B, Washington, CT, 52
15783 CLAY Timpson, Cherokee, NC, 31

EASTERN CHEROKEES RESIDING EAST OF MISSISSIPPI RIVER.

KEY: Guion Miller Application Number; Name; Address; Relation (to Head); Age in 1906

- **13863** CLEMONT, Mary M, Lindale, GA, 29; Callie, D, 5; Barnie, S, 4
- **26012** CLIFT, Nellie D, Soddy, TN, 35, RFD #3; Marie I, D, 6; Robert B, S, 6; Walter D, S, 1/12
- **15823** CLIMBINGBEAR, Ancy, Wahhiyah, NC, 28
- **12757** CLIMBINGBEAR, Daleeskee, Wahhiyah, NC, 31
- **15824** CLIMBINGBEAR, Katie, Swayney, NC, 17; By Ollie Climbingbear, Gdn
- **15829** CLIMBINGBEAR, Mabel, Wahhiyah, NC, 22
- **10033** CLIMBINGBEAR, Ollie, Wahhiyah, NC, 53
- **7924** CLINGAN, Edward E, Ooltewah, TN, 58; Elijah E, S, 13; Cherokee L, D, 11; William K, S, 2
- **12776** CLOUD, Sallie, Cherokee, NC, 83
- **16322** COCHRAN, Casey, Cherokee, NC, 72
- **16273** COCHRAN, Dorcus, Cherokee, NC, 58; Arch, S, 18; James, S, 17; Dehkie, S, 10
- **2307** COLDING, Letitia F, Savannah, GA, 76, 213 Thirty-second St
- **799** COLE, George W, Sweetgum, GA, 39; Ida, D, 15; Oma, D, 13; Evert, S, 10; Walter, S, 8; Jewel, D, 6; John, S, 2
- **802** COLE, Robert, Dora, GA, 30; Emery, Bro, 15; By Laura Cole, Gdn
- **796** COLE, William, Dora, GA, 26; Arlie, S, 1
- **123** COLLAKE, Crofford V, Mt Vernon, TN, 58
- **22397** COLLAKE, James, Mt Vernon, TN, 28; Bettie J, D, 5; William C, S, 1/12
- **22392** COLLAKE, Thomas G, Mt Vernon, TN, 28; Ora M, D, 3; Robert E, S, 1; Ada, D, 1/12
- **34633** COLONAHESKI, Abram, Carlisle, PA, 22, care Indian Industrial School
- **12782** COLANAHESKI, Isiah, Wahhiyah, NC, 56; Martha, D, 3; Mark, S, 1

[Colonahaskie, Jesse See #11151] *(Note: entry separate from other family groups)*

- **6414** COLONAH-HES-KIH or COLNESKEY, Tom, Robbinsville, NC, 19
- **45230** COMPTON, Omelie B, Columbus, GA,17, 212 16th St; Ann S, Sis, 14; Ellen H, Sis, 13; Shelby S, Bro, 10; Juliette H, Sis, 7; Mary K, Sis, 7; By Juliette CH Compton, Gdn
- **728** CONCENE, Jake, Robbinsville, NC, 70
- **6766** CONCENE, Manuel, Robbinsville, NC, 48
- **6767** CONCENE, Ona, Robbinsville, NC, 40
- **6768** CONCENE, Ropetwister, Robbinsville, NC,98
- **7746** CONLEY, John, Big Cove, NC, 46; 12753, Jennie, W, 48; 7746, John, Jr, S, 16; Luke, S, 11; Dorah, D, 3
- **10070** CONSEEN, Auganiah, Cherokee, NC, 65 [Died June, 1907]
- **10073** CONSEEN, Jack, Cherokee, NC, 21
- **2956** CONSEEN, Kate, Robbinsville, NC, 39; Martha, D, 11

[CONSEEN, Quakee See #8655] *(Note: entry separate from other family groups)*

- **2955** CONSEEN, Sallie, Tomotla, NC, 50   [Died 12 1907]
- **10071** CONSEEN, Sally, Cherokee, NC, 18
- **10072** CONSEEN, Thompson, Cherokee, NC, 22

EASTERN CHEROKEES RESIDING EAST OF MISSISSIPPI RIVER.

KEY: Guion Miller Application Number; Name; Address; Relation (to Head); Age in 1906

- **8602** CONSEENE, Dayunne, Robbinsville, NC 65
- **3962** CONSEENE, Nancy, Robbinsville, NC, 24
- **8599** CONSENE, Peter, Robbinsville, NC, 27; 8596, Nancy, W, 32
- **553** CONSTANT, Elizabeth, Ringgold, GA, 52
- **31250** CONSTANT, John B, Alton Park, TN, 28
- **31251** CONSTANT, Magnolia, Alton Park, TN, 24
- **15689** CON-TEES-KEE, Birdtown, NC, 61; 16300, Caroline, W, 59
- **21884** COOPER, Laura A, St Elmo, TN, 47
- **1482** COOPER, Mack, Andrews, NC, 26; Catherine L, D, ¾
- **8425** COOPER, Stacy Jane, Cherokee, NC, 39; Arnold, S, 13; Curdoas J, S, 11; Frankey N, S, 9; Celia Bell, D, 8; Fannie G, D, 6; Myrtle, D, 3; Fred W, S, 1
- **14220** CORN, Eliza M, Burtsboro, GA, 27; Mary M, D, 8; Elisha, S, 7; Frank, S, 5
- **425** CORNETT, Laura J, Cherrylog, GA, 36; Luther S, 8, 11; Luler M, D, 10; Ernest J, S, 7, Lora A, D, 5
- **15861** CORNSILK, Armstrong, Robbinsville, NC, 64, 8640 Annie, W, 48; 16020, Emeline, D, 19; 16019, Johnnie, S, 15; 16018, Hattie, D, 9; 16017, Howard, S, 6
- **16021** CORNSILK, Dow, Tomotla, NC, 26
- **16891** CORNSILK, Martha, Cheoah, NC, 22
- **12777** CORNSILK, York, Wahhiyah, NC, 39; 6211, E-yah-ni, W, 47; David, S, 17
- **23474** COWART, Nita See, Hill City, TN, 31, 300 Cowart St
- **628** COWART, Thomas, Hill City, TN, 60, 300 Cowart St
- **30328** CRAIG, Alice, Sudith, KY, 29; Roy, S, 8; Nadia, D, 6; Wiley, S, 3; Arvel, S, 1
- **8615** CRAIG, Georgie, Birdtown, NC, 23
- **8617** CRAIG, John, Birdtown, NC, 14; Frank, Bro, 12; By Joseph Craig, Gdn
- **8616** CRAIG, Mary, Birdtown, NC, 28; Robert D, S, 1
- **155** CRANE, Maria, Baltimore, MD, 53, 225 W Madison St
- **3228** CRANMORE, Amanda B, Soddy, TN, 30
- **18798** CROFT, John Lester, Blackwells, GA, 26
- **19343** CROFT, Joseph B, Marietta, GA, 37; John Henry, S, 16; Mary Lillie, D, 12; Minnie, D, 8; Joseph, S, 4
- **18799** CROFT, Martha E, Blackwells, GA, 22
- **18800** CROFT, Mary I, Blackwells, GA, 31
- **19344** CROFT, Minnie, Blackwells, GA, 19
- **19345** CROFT, Sarah E, Blackwells, GA, 57
- **15514** CROFT, William L, Marietta, GA, 34, RFD #8; Willie L, Jr, S, 2
- **1479** CROMWELL, Margaret P, Andrews, NC, 62
- **16801** CROW, Caroline, Cherokee, NC, 63
- **36154** CROW, David, Cherokee, NC, 21; 36553, Sallie, W, 17; Sam, S, 1

[Crow, Etta See #15704]
[Crow, Wesley See #15704] } *(Note: entries separate from other family groups)*

- **33905** CROW, Joe, Cherokee, NC, 39; 12779, Annie, W, 46; 33905, Minnie, D, 13; Boyd, S, 12
- **36155** CROW, John, Cherokee, NC, 24; 7752, Mary L, W, 22; 36155, Callie, D, 2
- **16890** CROW, Ossie, Cherokee, NC, 22

EASTERN CHEROKEES RESIDING EAST OF MISSISSIPPI RIVER.

KEY: Guion Miller Application Number; Name; Address; Relation (to Head); Age in 1906

43785 CROW, Robert, Cherokee, NC, 12; Dorg, Bro, 11; Luther, Bro, 9; Arthur, Bro, 9; Lossel, Bro, 7; Wesley, Bro, 17; By Mary A Crane, Gdn

[CROW, Wesley See #15704] *(Note: entry separate from other family groups)*

37364 CROW, Wesley R, Rosemont, PA, 29

[CROW, Wesley S See #34183] *(Note: entry separate from other family groups)*

21661 CROWDER, Lizzie, Rome, GA, 24, RFD #3, Box 9; Florence W, D, 5; Sedder B, S, 4; Kelsio M, S, 1/3
16327 CUCUMBER, Ar-gum-too-ga, Cherokee, NC,17; Arch, Bro, 18; 16327, Gun-to-gy, Bro, 10; By Dorcas Cucumber, Gdn
16845 CUCUMBER, Gena, Cherokee, NC, 26
39196 CUCUMBER, Katy, Cherokee, NC, 23; Saunooke, Ollie, S, 1
16844 CUCUMBER, Mose, Cherokee, NC, 30; 16326, Lilly, W, 20
16846 CUCUMBER, Willie, Cherokee, NC, 27
3960 CUNSEENE, Jim, Robbinsville, NC, 19; John, Bro, 15; Mary, Sis, 12; Donnie, Sis, 10; Willie, Bro, 7; By Breast Cunseene, Gdn
22956 CUPP, Pearl, Euchee, TN, 23, RFD (#?); Willie C, S, 2

11151 DAH-LE-YE-SKEE, Se-gil-lie, Cherokee, NC, 63; Co-lo-na-has-kie, Jesse, Ad S, 15
42562 DALE, John Thomas, Carbon Hill, AL, 17
42561 DALE, Willie, Collinsville, IL, 20
23196 DARNELL, Eliza, Dawsonville, GA, 51
20405 DAVIS, Arthur, Ooltewah, TN, 5; 20406, Lee, Bro, 7; 20481, Mamie, Sis, ¾; 20611 Mattie, Sis, 3; 20612, Nellie, Sis, 9; 20613, Clarence, Bro, 17; 20614, Willie, Bro, 15; By Sarah Jane Davis, Gdn
7747 DAVIS, Charley, Wahhiyah, NC, 36; 11134, Annie, W, 34; 7747, Israel, S, 12; Isaac, S, 9; David, S, 5; George, S, 1
6292 DAVIS, Cynthia, Norman, TN, 67; By Lafayette Davis, Gdn
10058 DAVIS, Dahick, Wahhiyah, NC, 56
1751 DAVIS, Daniel, Hedwig, GA, 60
5243 DAVIS, Daniel, Jr, Dahlonega, GA, 28; Dan C, S, 5; Rufe, S, 3; Lila Mary, D, 1
1835 DAVIS, Delilah J, Atlanta, GA, 58, 259 Rawson St
26458 DAVIS, Dock, Dahlonega, GA, 29; Clara, D, 8; Clinton, S, 6; Mattie, D, 4; Amanda, D, 2
1635 DAVIS, Earl, Dahlonega, GA, 45; Earl, Jr, S, 12; Miller, S, 11; Susan, D, 9; Stewart, S, 7; Julia, D, 4; Lee, S, 1
20616 DAVIS, Geo A, Ooltewah, TN, 29
20615 DAVIS, Jesse E, E Chattanooga, TN, 26; 209 Broad St
15862 DAVIS, Joe, Birdtown, NC, 36
6641 DAVIS, John, Wahhiyah, NC, 45; 6640 Annie, W, 52; Lizzie, D, 14
15713 DAVIS, Katy, Birdtown, NC, 54
18594 DAVIS, Kinney, Atlanta, GA, US Pen, 33

EASTERN CHEROKEES RESIDING EAST OF MISSISSIPPI RIVER.

KEY: Guion Miller Application Number; Name; Address; Relation (to Head); Age in 1906

- **6293** DAVIS, Lafayette, Harrison, TN, 60; Lillian, D, 19
- **2644** DAVIS, Lena L, Dahlonega, GA, 22
- **31220** DAVIS, Lena, Rossville, GA, 17
- **2705** DAVIS, Lorenzo D, Jr, Dahlonega, GA, 47; Bevilla G, D, 19; James G, S, 15; Frank, S, 15
- **1752** DAVIS, Lorenzo N, Hedwig, GA, 24; 1753, Jetta A, W, 25; Anstell N, S, 1
- **2470** DAVIS, Miller, Dahlonega, GA, 47; Mary L, D, 19; Sallie S, D, 17; Earl T, S, 15; Kate L, D, 4
- **10028** DAVIS, Quattie, Wahhiyah, NC, 70
- **986** DAVIS, Rebecca, Stonery, NC, 54
- **38318** DAVIS, Samuel L, Harrison, TN, 38
- **31183** DAVIS, Thos J, Harrison, TN, 28
- **5245** DAVIS, William, Dahlonega, GA, 41; Jefferson, S, 13
- **1754** DAVIS, William E, Hedwig, GA, 27; John H, S, 4; Luda, D, 2; Henley, S, 1
- **26009** DAVIS, William J, Retro, TN, 21
- **15694** DAVIS, Wilste, Birdtown, NC, 62; 15700, Alsie, W, 48; Caroline, D, 8
- **5968** DAY, Mattie A, Adairsville, KY, 26
- **11158** DEDAHLEEDOGEE, Annie, Wahhiyah, NC, 49
- **6203** DEDAHLEEDOGEE, Johnson, Wahhiyah, NC, 47; Wilson, S, 19; Sherman, S, 12; David, S, 10; Jim W, S, 8; Jona-ni, S, 5; Jackson, S, 3; Anna, D, 1/6
- **36951** DEGE, Charles F, Cincinnati, OH, 36; 418 Hopkins St
- **8652** DICKAGTISKA, Sallie, Robbinsville,NC,37
- **12756** DICKEN, Watson, Wahhiyah, NC, 55
- **41786** DICKEY, Ettie, Cherokee, NC, 25; Nannie, D, 1
- **806** DICKSON, Savannah G, Clayton, GA, 45
- **514** DICKSON, Stacy Cherokee, Clayton, GA,38; Maude, D, 15; Myrtle, D, 13; James R, S, 6
- **23696** DILLINGHAM, Bettie, Andrews, NC, 37
- **15782** DOBSON, John, Cherokee, NC, 90; 16827, Mary, W, 54
- **30525** DOCKERY, Emma, Murphy, NC, 25; Eliza, D, 1
- **513** DOCKINS, Tobitha, Clayton, GA, 47
- **5270** DOUGHERTY, Ben, Murrayville, GA, 25, RFD #10; Seaborn, S, 1
- **24798** DOUGHERTY, Charles E, Cumming, GA, 45; Homer, S, 19; Hillard, S, 17; Lora, D, 15; Lizzie, D, 15
- **3754** DOUGHERTY, John H, Landrum, GA, 33
- **28786** DOUGHERTY, Romania, Murryville, GA, 11, RFD #2; Polina, Sis, 9; Allie, Sis, 5; By Ben Dougherty, Gdn
- **332** DOUGHERTY, Susan J, Cumming GA, 64

[Downing, Arch See #19730] *(Note: entry separate from other family groups)*

- **6632** DOWNING, Sally, Cherokee, NC, 52
- **10038** DRIVER, Abraham, Wahhiyah, NC, 31
- **29681** DRIVER, Chickalee B, Swayney, NC, 24; 15818, Allie, W, 22; 29681, Rosa, D, 6; George, S, 3; Samuel, S, 1
- **11110** DRIVER, Dick, Wahhiyah, NC, 61; Nannie, D, 1

EASTERN CHEROKEES RESIDING EAST OF MISSISSIPPI RIVER.

KEY: Guion Miller Application Number; Name; Address; Relation (to Head); Age in 1906

11128 DRIVER, Eliza, Cherokee, NC, 36; Ned, S, 7; Adam, S, 4; Lucy, D, 1
28957 DRIVER, Goliath, Carlisle, PA, 30
15820 DRIVER, James, Wahhiyah, NC, 74; 15819, Quattie, W, 65
29689 DRIVER, Judas B, Swayney, NC, 40; 29688 , Eliza, S, 40
27484 DRIVER, Lossil, Newtown, PA, 28; Marion, S, #
29926 DRIVER, Wesley, Swayney NC,36; 29927, Acgeenee, W, 37; John, S, 13; Lucinda, D, 9
11126 DRIVER, Will, Cherokee, NC, 34
11155 DUNCAN, Lillian V, Cherokee, NC, 30; Potter, Tommy, S, 11; Duncan, Subal, D, 1
13186 DUNLAP, Alice, Bryson City, NC, 22
13185 DUNLAP, Berry, Bryson City, NC, 19
13184 DUNLAP, Robert, Bryson City, NC, 15

5290 EDMONDS, Robert, Soddy TN, 24; Eumille, D, 2
5292 EDMONDS, Thomas, Soddy, TN, 6; By Pink Edmonds, Gdn
33364 ELLIOTT, John, Knoxville, TN, 31; Gracie, D, 2
25049 ELLISON, Minnie, Dayton, TN, 20; John, S, 1/6
15805 ENOLA, Don, Cherokee, NC, 56
20582 ERVIN, Maggie, Chattanooga, TN, 24, 1424 Cowart St; Willard, S, 1; Claud, S, 4

[Etter, Sarah V See Western Roll]   *(Note: entry separate from other family groups)*

29197 EUBANKS, Roger Roy, Chicago, IL, 27, 1311 Mich Ave or Pryor Creek OK; 34072, Martha L W, 27
2732 EVANS, Mary Ann, Marblehill, GA, 28; Tate, S, 7; Horner, S, 5; Elmer, S, 5; Bonnie, D, 2

7817 FAUCETT, Nancy, Tate, GA, 35; Irene, D, ¼
10027 FEATHER, Lawyer, Cherokee, NC, 39; 12748, Mary, W, 38; Ge-law-mi-je, S,10; Annie, D, 8; Nancy, D, 6; Jonah, S, 1; Wa-hoo, Elsie, D of W, 19
15790 FEATHERHEAD, Wilson, Cherokee, NC, 30; 15803, Nancy, W, 72
554 FIELDS, John, Chattanooga, TN, 69
21 FINGER, Sophria C, Louisville, TN, 32; Ramona I, D, 11; Samuel A, S, 9; Leona A, D, 2
1445 FOSTER, Alcy, Culberson, NC, 32; Alcy, D, 7; Robert, S, 5; Burton, S, 3; Lee Roy, S, 1/3

[FREELAND, Martha C See #2713]
[FREELAND, William H See #2713]   *(Note: entries separate from other family groups)*
[FREELAND, Ida L See #2713]
[FREELAND, Delia H See #2713]

12996 FRENCH, Awee S, Birdtown, NC, 32; Maud, D, 12; Maronie, D, 9; Morgan, S, 7; Soggie, S, 5; George B, S, 2

EASTERN CHEROKEES RESIDING EAST OF MISSISSIPPI RIVER.

KEY: Guion Miller Application Number; Name; Address; Relation (to Head); Age in 1906

[FRENCH, Ross See #16301]   *(Note: entry separate from other family groups)*

14636 FRENCH, Wallie, Whittier, NC, 27; Charlotte, D, 13; Ella Nona, D, 10; Ned, S, 9; Maggie, D, 7; Nellie Maria D, 5; Jesse, S, 2

34307 GANN, Allen, Soddy TN, 22; Raymond, S, 1/8
34306 GANN, Henry, Soddy, TN, 20
5291 GANN, Robert R, Soddy, TN, 39; Elliott, Stella Pearl, D, 18; Maning, Maimi Ethel, 15; Gann, Gertie, D, 12; James R, S, 9; William T, S, 5; Robert A, S, 1
3227 GANN, William T, Soddy TN, 50
3198 GARLAND, Elizabeth, Culberson, NC, 76
3195 GARLAND, Jesse T, Culberson, NC, 50; Addie T, D, 17; Jessie M, D, 15; Emery, S 4; Rodie, D, 1
3686 GARLAND, John B, Culberson, NC, 28
3683 GARLAND, Lonza, Culberson, NC, 21
3197 GARLAND, Roxanna, Culberson, NC, 48
3687 GARLAND, Tullis B, Culberson, NC, 56
3196 GARLAND, William S, Culberson, NC, 40
3707 GARMONY, Jane S, Chattanooga, TN, 39, 123 Mitchel St
27152 GARRARD, Mary E, Higdon, AL, 26; John E, S, 4; James W, S, 2; Eliza A, D, 1
19082 GARRETT, Lou, Cumming, GA, 36; 19083, Mary D, 16; Ola, D, 13; Van, S, 10; Dovey, D, 8; Calvin, S, 4
34097 GASPARETTI, Mary Ann, Collinsville, IL 30; Johnny, S, 11; Thomas, S, 10; Catharine, D, 7; Victor, S, 5; Raphael, S, 3
20064 GASTON, Charles, Cleveland, TN, 19, RFD #6; Martha, Sis, 18; Allie, Sis, 16; By TL Gaston, Gdn
20257 GEARING, Eliza, Commerce, GA, 36
15838 GEORGE, Alsie Bearmeat, Birdtown, NC,24
28502 GEORGE, Annie, Philadelphia, PA, 22, 1800 Arch St
16267 GEORGE, Davis, Cherokee, NC, 57
12761 GEORGE, Dawson, Whittier, NC, 45; 12749, Mary, W, 45; Manly, S, 19; Martha, D, 15; Ollie, D, 11
16802 GEORGE, Elijah, Cherokee, NC, 34; 16830, Quatie, W, 32; Cain, S, 10; Lewis, S, 2; Agnes, D, 10; Green, S, 6
39476 GEORGE, Elijah, Cherokee, NC, 27
15799 GEORGE, Joe Stone, Birdtown, NC, 48; 15802, Lizzie, W, 40; Lizer, D, 17; Jacob, S, 12; Celie, D, 7; Jackson, S, 4
24438 GEORGE, Judas, Birdtown, NC, 26, [Died 10-06-?]; Elmore Don, S, 3; Sallie Ann, D, 1/3 [Died 6-17-1906]; Alsie George, Gdn And Adm
11142 GEORGE, Julia V, Silver Creek, NY, 31; Charlotte B, D, 2
24442 GEORGE, Lindy, Birdtown, NC, 20
14740 GEORGE, Logan, Cherokee, NC, 12; JOHNSON, Simon, Cous, 12; By James Johnson, Uncle and Gdn
16255 GEORGE, Nancy, Cherokee, NC, 64
15800 GEORGE, Yonaskin, Birdtown, NC, 52; 24469, Nancy, W, 40; Mark, S, 14; Annie, D, 11

EASTERN CHEROKEES RESIDING EAST OF MISSISSIPPI RIVER.

KEY: Guion Miller Application Number; Name; Address; Relation (to Head); Age in 1906

12760 GEORGE, Shell, Cherokee, NC, 47
16254 GEORGE, Shon, Cherokee, NC, 32
16288 GEORGE, Suttawage, Cherokee, NC, 64; 16805, Ester, W, 48
2713 GIBBONS, Cordelia, Marble, NC, 41; FREELAND, Martha, D, 16; William H, S, 20; Ida L, D, 13; Delia H, D, 13; Lane, Clark, S, 5
962 GILL, Calsina, Rockwood, TN, 4
10978 GILLESPIE, Tennessee, Highland Park, TN, 50; Marcus E, S, 16; Grace, D, 12; William R, S, 10; James R, S, 8; John W, S, 8
31260 GOBLE, Benjamin ML, Albertville, AL, 42, RFD 33; James, S, 21 (Name marked through); Louvina, D, 20; Bert, S, 17; Nancy, D, 14; Colquitt, S, 12; Arvel, S, 9; Lee, S, 7; Louis, S, 5; Harley, S, 3
2264 GOBLE, George W, Quarles, GA, 32; Madelphia, D, 6; July, D, 4; Henry, S, 2; Joseph, S, ¼
31262 GOBLE, James L, Albertville, AL, 22
31263 GOBLE, John W, Boaz, AL, 34; Emma, D, 15; Leonard, S, 12; Duncan, S, 10; May, D, 8; Mollie, D, 4; Harvey, S, 1
24 GOBLE, Liza, Boaz, AL, 27; John, S, 5; Hershal, S, 3; Earl, S, 2
1521 GOBLE, Nancy, Quarles, GA, 76
23890 GOFORTH, Minnie, Birdtown, NC, 19
6762 GOINS, Ban, Robbinsville, NC, 40
20563 GOINS, Henry, Chattanooga, TN, 26, 606 Sydna St
6644 GOINS, James, Sevierville, TN, 75
15841 GOINSNAKE, Nancy, Birdtown, NC, 56; Stephen, S, 18
11240 GOLECH, Maggie, Cherokee, NC, 17
31908 GOSS, Amy, Dawsonville, GA, 32; Lella M, D, 14; Clarice E, D, 12; Bonnie Lynn, S, 10; Ethel A, D, 8; Bennie K, S, 4; Ernest, S, 2
17738 GOSSETT, Mary, St Elmo, TN, 36, 804 Harris St; 20626, Ardealy, D, 9; 20623, William, S, 7; 20625, Albert, S, 6; 20624, Harry, S, 3; 20629, Earnest, S, 14; 20628, Lena, D, 12; 20627, Viola, D, 10

[GRASSHOPPER, Jarrett See #26246] *(Note: entry separate from other family groups)*

[GRASSHOPPER, Will See #3948] [Died 12-27-1907]
(Note: entry separate from other family groups)

26177 GRAVITT, Emma, Plainsville, GA, 21
7620 GRAVITT, George W, Plainsville, GA, 55; Brite, S, 19; Susie, D, 17; Pearl, D, 13; James, S, 7
7619 GRAVITT, John, Plainsville, GA, 61; Thomas, S, 19; Carrie, D, 17; Lolie, D, 14; Norris, S, 12
26406 GRAVITT, Lester, Plainsville, GA 25; Cora, D, 1
26405 GRAVITT, Oconel, Plainsville, GA, 21
7618 GRAVITT, Pollie, Plainsville, GA, 50
7617 GRAVITT, Thomas, Plainsville, GA, 55; Willie, S, 18; Hallie, D, 15
33020 GRAYBEARD, Ezekial, Marble, NC, 66
9894 GRAYBEARD, Lillie, Robbinsville, NC, 15

EASTERN CHEROKEES RESIDING EAST OF MISSISSIPPI RIVER.

KEY: Guion Miller Application Number; Name; Address; Relation (to Head); Age in 1906

7652 GRAYBEARD, Sallie, Cherokee, NC, 8; James, Bro, 5; By Hazeltine Money Gdn
9895 GRAYBEARD, Stacy, Robbinsville, NC, 17
27868 GREEN Cora Elizabeth, Letitia, NC, 22
23976 GREEN, Minnie B, Charleston, TN, 28; Andrew, S, 12; Thomas, S, 10; Henry, S, 1
5481 GREYBEARD, Aggie, Marble, NC, 58
32347 GRIFFITH, Addie, Oliver Springs, TN, 46

5295 HAIL, David W, Decatur, TN, 59
24294 HAIL, John F, Decatur, TN, 25
24293 HAIL, Kittie, Decatur, TN, 34
24292 HAIL, Ninnie, Decatur, TN, 30
14775 HALL, Ethel Eveline, Savannah, GA, 24, 228 E Park Ave
22398 HAMILTON, Lizzie, Mt Vernon, TN, 20; Myrtle, D, 1
22393 HAMILTON, Martha, Mt Vernon, TN, 31
37200 HANCOCK, Donald C, Rome, GA, 22
12178 HANCOCK, Sallie E, Rome, GA, 39; Ralph J, S, 17; Glennis R, S, 11
14218 HANCOCK, Sarah J, Avondale, AL, 51, 4024 1st Ave, N
2777 HANNAH, Dave F, Sherman Heights, TN, 40; Mary White, D, 7; Alva Reter, S, 5; Jessie Lee, D, 2; Joseph Columbus, S, ¾
2774 HANNAH, Jack W, Chattanooga, TN, 36; 19628, Beulah H, D, 13; Sophia Lee, D, 10; Mary Cecil, D, 8
2774 HANNAH, James M, E Chattanooga, TN,33; 20194, Marvin M, S, 2; James E, S, 1½; Pauline M, D, 4½ [Died 12-1906]
20196 HANNAH, Wallace P, Chattanooga, TN, 18; Jack W, Bro, 16; By Jas M Hannah, Actg Gdn
1954 HARALSON, Susan D, Atlanta, GA, 52, 137 Spring St
3902 HARDIN, Celia, Andrews, NC, 12
2653 HARDIN, Cain, Andrews, NC, 31; William H, S, 2; Grant, S, 1
2660 HARDIN, Charles H, Andrews, NC, 36; James W, S, 15; Richard S, S, 13; Anna E, D, 11; Thomas J, S, 10; Lillian M, D, 8; Belvia AL, D, 5; Verdia E, D, 2
3965 HARDIN, Dock, Andrews, NC, 20
3967 HARDIN, Dolphus, Andrews, NC, 25; James O, S, 3; Arnis E, D, 1
687 HARDIN, Elizabeth, Andrews, NC, 60
2896 HARDIN, Frank J, Andrews, NC, 29; Willie P, S, 8; Dillard, S, 5; Oden, S, 3; Hubbard, S, 1
3972 HARDIN, Loyd, Andrews, NC, 22; Pearley, D, 3; Romelus, S, 1
3903 HARDIN, Mattie, Andrews, NC, 14
2654 HARDIN, William J, Andrews, NC, 32; Sattie, D, 12; Lousine, D, 10; Virge, D, 8; Hardie, S, 6; Roy, S, 2
13342 HARMAN, Ellen C, Savannah, GA, 36; Julie C, D, 5; George L, Jr, S, 2
13006 HARRIS, Benjamin H, Wolf Creek, NC, 26
17365 HARRIS, Mindo Black, Cartersville, GA, 25, RFD #4; Romeo, S, 6; Raymond, S, 4; Bertha, D, 2
24398 HARRIS, Ollie, Whittier, NC, 33

EASTERN CHEROKEES RESIDING EAST OF MISSISSIPPI RIVER.

KEY: Guion Miller Application Number; Name; Address; Relation (to Head); Age in 1906

33088 HANKINS, Daisey, Cotton Mills, GA, 23
4535 HAWKINS, Dora, Culberson, NC, 25;Charles, S, 3
24324 HENRY, Hubert P, Guntersville, AL, 24
23888 HENRY, Hugh B, Guntersville, All 49
25184 HENRY, Joseph J, Memphis, TN, 17; 82 Market Ave
24325 HENRY, Robert G, Guntersville, AL, 18
30273 HENSLEY, Arthur, Tellico Plains, TN, 28; Claud, S, 1
5420 HENSLEY, Emma Jane, Carters, GA, 44; James Robert, S, 19; Ellen Lena, D, 16; Ida M, D, 14; Arthur J, S, 11; Grace P D, 2
36303 HENSLEY, Estela May, Caters, Ga, 21
5421 HENSLEY, John Luther, Goble, GA, 22
30274 HENSLEY, JV, Tellico Plains, TN, 27
743 HENSLEY, Mary J, Tellico Plains, TN, 51; Nora, D, 16; Emma, D, 11
24038 HENSON, Mary A, Chattanooga, TN, 62, 12 Mechanic St
31264 HIGGINS, Lavina, Boaz, AL, 37 [insane], By Starling Higgins (next friend), RFD #3
2627 HIGGINS, Noah, Rome, GA, 37; 2627, Gracy, D, 14; Mylus, S, 16; Zollie, D, 8; Ollie, D, 8
31258 HIGGINS, Starling V, Boaz, AL, 36, Box 4,, RFD #3; Georgia VM, D, 14; Lee, S, 8; Berney B, S, 6; Nellie P, D, 3
1255 HILDEBRAND, Amelia E, Benton, TN, 65
1254 HILDEBRAND, Eliza Jane, Benton, TN, 63
1256 HILDEBRAND, John W, Benton, TN, 88
3537 HILDEBRAND, Lawrence, Benton, TN, 60?
3536 HILDEBRAND, Lawrence W, Jr, Benton, TN, 35; Lawrence, 3rd, S, 1/24
6200 HILL, Abraham, Wahhiyah, NC, 46; 6220, Annie, W, 38
11109 HILL, Ann, Wahhiyah, NC, 63; Nancy, D, 14; Hausley, S, 8; Kelley, S, 4
39478 HILL, Blaine, Wahhiyah, NC, 20
17366 HILL, Moda Black, Cartersville, GA, 17
42126 HILL, Soggy M, Wahhiyah, NC, 26; 29401, Henrietta C, W, 33
11111 HILL, John, Wahhiyah, NC, 55; 11106, Sallie, W, 80
16025 HILL, Maul, Wahhiyah, NC, 57; Ned, S, 19; Levi, S, 17; Caroline, D, 13
2401 HILL, Oden C, Perryville, WV, 23; Gudger G, S, 1/12
18989 HIX, Sarah, Gainesville, GA, 47, RFD #10
13991 HOLLAND, Jennie S, Cherokee, NC, 20
4143 HOLLINGSWORTH, Iley A, High Point, GA, 15
29080 HOPKINS, Mary M, Lawrenceville, GA, 25
13797 HORNBUCKLE, Davis, Birdtown, NC, 45; Jefferson, S, 19
15844 HORNBUCKLE, Elvira, Cherokee, NC, 9; Jules, Bro, 7; By George Hornbuckle, Gdn
6635 HORNBUCKLE, George, Cherokee, NC, 29; Malissa, D, 10; Alice May, D, 8; Hartman, S, 5; Olive Ann, D, 3; John Russell, S, 1
10806 HORNBUCKLE, Henry, Birdtown, NC, 46 [Dec'd]
10031 HORNBUCKLE, Israel, Cherokee, NC, 20
15811 HORNBUCKLE, John, Cherokee, NC, 33; 15806, Martha, W, 43; Ollie, D, 7; Donny, S, 5

EASTERN CHEROKEES RESIDING EAST OF MISSISSIPPI RIVER.

KEY: Guion Miller Application Number; Name; Address; Relation (to Head); Age in 1906

39475 HORNBUCKLE, John Lewis, Cherokee, NC, 23
7651 HORNBUCKLE, Johnson, Almond, NC, 5; Andy, Bro, 2; Ben, Bro, ¾; By Sallie Catt, Gdn
14743 HORNBUCKLE, Lewis, Cherokee, NC, 51; 16806, Caroline, W, 52
11113 HORNBUCKLE, Maggie, Cherokee NC, 26
11114 HORNBUCKLE, Rebecca, Cherokee, NC, 66
6649 HORNBUCKLE, William, Cherokee, NC, 38; Addie, D, 12; Fred, S, 10; Dora, D, 7; Wilson, S, 4; Maggie, D, 1
10042 HORNBUCKLE, William, Cherokee, NC, 25
26406 HOUK, Manerva, Plainsville, GA, 36; Benson, S, 15; Cormitha, D, 11; Carl, S, 8; Dorsey, S, 5; Lillie, D, 3
15193 HOWELL, Charles Henry, Chattanooga, TN, 37; 15181, Mary Elizabeth, D, 5; 15184, Emily K, D, 2
2253 HOWELL, Ellen E, New York City, NY, 47, 69 48th St
29 HOWELL, Emily C, Marietta, GA, 70
14659 HOWELL, Emily Kate, Chattanooga, TN, 53, 461 Oak St
15754 HOWELL, Eston E, Chattanooga, TN, 33, 418 Oak St,
1525 HOWELL, Evan C, Marietta, GA, 27, 312 Kennesaw Ave
15880 HOWELL, Frank R, Chattanooga, TN, 29
14656 HOWELL,JamesCleland,Chattanooga,TN,57, 461 Oak St
3230 HOWELL, Joseph B, Pendergrass, GA, 49; Ralph, S, 17; Ernest G, S, 15; Herbert T, S, 7; Callie M, D, 4
18514 HOWELL, Julia B, Marietta, Ga, 42, 312 Kennesaw Ave
14658 HOWELL, Letitia Pooler, Chattanooga, TN, 50

[HOWELL, Luther See #13881]   *(Note: entry separate from other family groups)*

37 HOWELL, Mary Davis, Marietta, GA, 36, 312 Kennesaw Ave
15876 HOWELL, Robert EL, Marietta, GA, 40; 312 Kennesaw Ave
35903 HOWELL, Samuel M, Riceville, TN, 57; William, S, 17; Loranzie, D, 11; Lucy, D, 9; Lee, S, 5; Bessy, D, 1
15760 HOWELL, Stephen Elliott, Chattanooga, Tn, 54, 418 Oak St; 15759, Emily Collier, D, 16; 15884, Samuel W, S, 13
15758 HOWELL, Thomas C, Chattanooga, TN, 30?; 418 Oak St
3231 HOWELL, William, DP, Dahlonetga, GA,57
2891 HUGGINS, Martha A, Young Harris, GA 41; Julia A, D, 19; John H, S, 17; Sarah N, D, 14; Lizzie, D, 11
5377 HUGHES, Eliza A, Roswell, GA, 62
12141 HUGHES,, Fanny M, Lynchburg, VA, 42, 712 Court St; ALEXANDER, Geo M, Lynchburg, VA,17, 1000 Court St; Jeanie M, D, 14
5376 HUGHES, Robert A, Roswell, Ga, 36; Clarence W, S, 15; Horace C, S, 11; Gladys M, D, 8; Courtney C, S, 4; Laura L, D, 1
25040 HULSEY, Alvin Alonzo, Dougherty, GA, 35; Andrew Carl, S, 10; Annie Maud, D, 9; Henry Allen, S, 7; John Priestly, S, 5; Sarah Isabel, D, 3; Lena, D, 2
32956 HULSEY, Charley M, Hoschton, GA, 24
5056 HULSEY, Sarah, Dougherty, GA, 48, [Died 12-27-1907]; Conrad L, S, 19

EASTERN CHEROKEES RESIDING EAST OF MISSISSIPPI RIVER.

KEY: Guion Miller Application Number; Name; Address; Relation (to Head); Age in 1906

25437 HULSEY, William R, Dougherty, GA, 21
10807 HYDEN, Emma L, Atlanta, GA, 30, 54 Jackson St

15779 IKE, Sam, Cherokee, NC, 57
22395 ISBILL, Sarah A, Madisonville, TN,30, RR #5; Lillie M, D, 4; Mary I, D, 2; Isabell, D, 1/12

15863 JACK, Nancy, Birdtown, NC, 68
6025 JACKSON, Fox Squirrel, Robinsville, NC,51; Jacob, S, 13

[JACKSON, Jack See #11139] *(Note: entry separate from other family groups)*

6653 JACKSON, John, Cherokee, NC, 69; 6637, Stacy, W, 42
12976 JACKSON, Jonas, Birdtown, NC, 24
3954 JACKSON, Lawyer, Robbinsville, NC, 34; 3955, Dakie or Takie, W, 37; Ella, D, 12; Florence, D, 5
10067 JACKSON, Ollie, Birdtown, NC, 46
6023 JACKSON, Robert, Robbinsville, NC, 31; 6022, Caroline, W, 28; Wesley, S, 6; David, S, 4; Edward, S, 2
17556 JACKSON, Sarah, Cherokee, NC, 28
15877 JENKINS, Marcoda, Tailscreek, GA, 22

[JESSANN, Sim De Hart See #12764] *(Note: entry separate from other family groups)*

[JESSON, Lydia J and Joe See #6642] *(Note: entry separate from other family groups)*

15018 JOEREE, Dahonala J, Cherokee, NC, 27; 10064, Mary, W, 17
10039 JOHNERIWAYNE, Cherokee, NC, 23
14742 JOHNSON, Addison, Harrisburg, PA, 21, 353 Hummel St
16253 JOHNSON, Caroline, Cherokee, NC, 59
13861 JOHNSON, China, Spring Place, GA, 40; Charlie M, S, 17
28592 JOHNSON, Cider, Birdtown, NC, 29
28781 JOHNSON, Go-lin-die, Birdtown, NC, 21
14739 JOHNSON, James, Cherokee, NC, 46
15786 JOHNSON, Jimpsie, Cherokee, NC, 34
16271 JOHNSON, Lunchi, Cherokee, NC, 54
15843 JOHNSON, Stephen, Birdtown, NC, 64; 12764, Jennie, W, 57; Skeeg, S, 19; JESSANN, Sim De Hart, GS, 3

[JOHNSON, Thomas C See #23475]
[JOHNSON, James N See #23475] *(Note: entries separate from other family groups)*
[JOHNSON, Richard C See #23457]
[JOHNSON, Anna R See #23457]

36937 JOHNSON, Yona, Cherokee, NC, 26; 9998, Dora, W, 22
7756 JO-LA-OO-GO-OOTH, Amy, Ocona Lufty, NC, 50

EASTERN CHEROKEES RESIDING EAST OF MISSISSIPPI RIVER.

KEY: Guion Miller Application Number; Name; Address; Relation (to Head); Age in 1906

22491 JONES, Annie C, Roswell, GA, 24; Mary R, D, 6; James H, S, 3
 6643 JOREE, Jessan, Cherokee, NC, 70; 6642, Lydia, W, 46; Joe, S, 10
16323 JUMPER, Ella, Cherokee, NC, 54
15766 JUMPER, Ute, Cherokee, NC, 35; 15767, Betsy, W, 36; Stancie, S, 7; Edward, S, 6; James, S, 3; Thomas, S, 1
15684 JUNULUSKIE, Birdtown, NC, 15, By Katy Davis, Gdn

17126 KANOUGHT, Abel, Japan, NC, 25
17127 KANOUGHT, Columbus, Birdtown, NC, 23
 6634 KEG, James, Birdtown, NC, 65; 6633, Katie, W, 56
15709 KEGG, Modiah, Birdtown, NC, 42
 5400 KELL, Alexander, Kyle, GA, 37
 2901 KELL, Andy, Blue Ridge, GA, 41; Richard, S, 18; Florida, D, 15; Effa, D, 9; Lucinda, D, 8; Oran, S, 5
 2027 KELL, Bryson, Blue Ridge, GA, 13; Arthur B, Bro, 8; By Mary E Buchanan, Gdn
34001 KELL, Ida, Blue Ridge, GA, 20
18762 KELL, Susanna, Blue Ridge, GA, 40
 1779 KEY, Samantha N, Cherrylog, GA, 24; Laney C, S, 4; William C, S, 1
29453 KEYS, Reed M, Houser, AL, 23
 7520 KEYS, William S, Houser AL: 57; STONER, Willie E, GS, 5; Thelma T, GD, 3
29454 KEYS, Willie Maud, Houser, AL, 25; KEYS, Texas C, D, 16
 7594 KIDD, David, Grape Creek, NC, 40; Walter, S, 17; De, S, 14; William, S, 10; Wesley, S, 6; Luther, S, 3
13878 KIRBY, Margaret, Spring Place, GA, 34; William, S, 5
11273 KIRKLAND, Martha L YellowCreek,NC,47; Georgia E, D, 5
24576 KNOUGHT, Sonsey, Japan, NC, 22

 6648 LAMBERT, Albert J, Cherokee, NC, 52
11154 LAMBERT, Charley, Swayney, NC, 21; 15859, Mary, W, 20; Jackson, S, 1/3
39516 LAMBERT, Edward, Ocona Lufty, NC, 21
10023 LAMBERT, Hugh, Birdtown, NC, 32; Pearley, D, 8; Jack, S, 6; Isaac, S, 4
11207 LAMBERT, Hugh, Forney, AL, 25; Lee F, S, 2
34381 LAMBERT, Hugh N, Cherokee, NC, 26; 7732, Alice RL, W, 22; William H, S, 1
26832 LAMBERT, Jackson, Cherokee NC, 22; Lula, D, 1
11122 LAMBERT, James M, Ocona Lufty, NC, 50; Capter Moses, S, 20; Minnie Hester, D, 18; Charles Jackson, S, 16; George Fred, S, 13; Jesse James, S, 11; Fritz Simmes, S, 9
26830 LAMBERT, James W, Cherokee, NC, 31; Bessie A, D, 7; Hugh H, S, 5
26833 LAMBERT, Jessie, Cherokee, NC, 30
10049 LAMBERT, John N, Cherokee, NC, 44
 6506 LAMBERT, Loyd, Birdtown, NC, 22;16332, Sallie,W,27; Luzena, D,5; Ollianna, D, 2
12780 LAMBERT, Pierson, Cherokee, NC, 6; By Lucy A Murphy, Gdn
11206 LAMBERT, Roscoe, Forney, AL, 31; Albert, S, 9; Georgia, D, 7; William, S, 6; Andrew, S, 4; Finley, S, 2

EASTERN CHEROKEES RESIDING EAST OF MISSISSIPPI RIVER.

KEY: Guion Miller Application Number; Name; Address; Relation (to Head); Age in 1906

10048 LAMBERT, Samuel, Cherokee, NC, 47; Clauda, D, 16; Nannie G, D, 14; Verdie, D, 12; Corbett, S, 10; Cora Lee, D, 8; Julia F, D, 6; Theodora R, D, 4
30850 LAMBERT, Thomas, Birdtown, NC, 27; Joseph, S, 4; Herman, S, 3; John, S, 2
25854 LAMBERT, Thomas R, Ocona Lufty, NC,23
11209 LAMBERT, Tilden, Forney, AL, 29
11506 LANCE, Mary V, Dalton, GA, 45; John M, S, 15; Joseph M, S, 9; Thomas J, S, 6
26006 LANCE, Mary E, Retro, TN, 27; Ira D, S, 2
26407 LANGLEY, Alfred A, Plainsville, GA, 30; Wheeler, S, 8; George, S, 5; Charles, S, 3
26407 LANGLEY, Ann, Plainsville, GA, 60; Mollie, D, 15; Nora Dell, D, 19
4832 LANGLEY, Columbus C, Whitestone,GA,21
7610 LANGLEY, Warren M, Calhoun, GA, 38; Essie, D, 17; Mattie, D, 15; May, D, 12; Robert, S, 5; William, S, 2
2449 LANGLEY, William A, Rober, GA, 53; Walter, S, 16; Augustus, S, 17; Eulena J, D, 14; Mary M, D, 13; Lilley May, D, 9; Mauda Lee, D, 6; Missa, D, 2
4829 LANGLEY, William T, Whitestone, GA, 17
16290½ LARCHEE, Daniel, Cherokee, NC, 66
4830 LANGLEY, Vinia, Whitestone, GA, 17; Della, Sis, 16; Chesley, Bro, 14; Amanda, Sis, 13; Sarah, Sis, 11; Lizzie, Sis 10; Elma, Sis, 10; By Josephine Langley, Gdn
2513 LANGSTON, Rosa Lee, Cass Station, GA, 35; Walter R, S, 17; William A, S, 15; Bessie F, D, 13; Esther L, D, 8; Ollie M, D, 4; Dixie Lee, D, 1
4359 LAWRENCE, Chas Colding,Marietta,GA,32
7753 LAWSON, Charlie, Big Cove, NC, 47; 7755, Jennie, W, 38; Dave L S, 13; Thompson, S, 11; Kannada, S, 7; Johnyasie, S, 3; Hayes, S, 1
29674 LAWSON, Leandy, Swayney, NC, 22
1575 LEADFORD, Catherine M, Culberson, NC, 32; Iowa, D, 13; Minnie, D, 11; Cora, D, 4; Adkins, S, 1
1767 LEATHERWOOD, Addie, BlueRidge,GA,32; Coreine G, D, 13; Luther, S, 11; Lela, D, 99
16842 LEDFORD, Annie, Almond, NC, 60
16848 LEDFORD, Charley, Tomotla, NC, 24; Allenie, D, 2
16849 LEDFORD, Jacke, Almond, NC, 33; 16299, Mary, W, 29; Moses, S, 4; John, S, 2; Lucyan, D, 1/12
12115 LEDFORD, Riley, Almond, NC, 28; Joe, S, 6; Kiney, S, 4; Eave, D, 1
16847 LEDFORD, Sampson, Robbinsville, NC, 21
12118 LEE, Alonzo, Silver Creek, NY, 32; Alice M, D, 5
11144 LEE, Laura Ann, Birdtown, NC, 43; Samuel, S, 17; Oberlander, S, 14; Edith, D, 12; Debrader, S, 10
3684 LEFEVERS, Temoxyenah, Culberson, NC,25; Linnie, D, 7; William E, S, 5
11208 LEMINGS, Nannie, Forney, AL, 27; Ollie, S, 2
34955 LENOIR, Henry Clifton, Pink, AL, 22
34954 LENOIR, John Albert, Pink, All 56, RFD #1; Annie, D, 19; Daisy, D, 17; Lula, D, 10; Mamie, D, 6; Edgar, S, 2; May, D, 1/12
13206 LENOIR, Thomas R, Savannah, GA,22, C/o Mrs MJ Lenoir; Cor Park Ave & Lincoln St,

EASTERN CHEROKEES RESIDING EAST OF MISSISSIPPI RIVER.

KEY: Guion Miller Application Number; Name; Address; Relation (to Head); Age in 1906

 7831 LEWIS, Henry W, Holly Springs, GA, 30; Myrtle, D, 4; Irene, D, 2; Mable E, D, 1/3
 7833 LEWIS, James W, Holly Springs, GA, 28
 7834 LEWIS, Thomas A, Kennesaw, GA, 37; Maley, D, 9 ; Estelle, D, 7; Christine, D, 5; John E, S, 4; Fred N, S, 2
12795 LITTLEJOHN, Elowih, Cherokee, NC, 28

[LITTLEJOHN, Mary See #10021] *(Note: entry separate from other family groups)*

17204 LITTLEJOHN, Sounooke, Cherokee, NC, 44; 15792, Annie E, W, 37; Wiggins, S, 15; Mindy, D, 13; Henson, S, 8; John, S, 5; Owen, S, 1
 6189 LITTLEJOHN, Twister, Cherokee, NC, 41; 6651, Annie, W, 29; Sallie, D, 3; Ike, S, 5/12
42919 LITTLEJOHN, Will, Cherokee, NC, 38; Gion, S, 10; Kate, D, 7; Isaac, S, 6; Garrett, S, 1
11124 LOCUST, John, Cherokee, NC, 58; 6198, Polly Ann, W, 56
26249 LOCUST, John, Brady, NC, 26
10026 LOCUST, Noah, Whittier, NC, 26; Louis McK, S, 5; Lomie B, D, 3; Tennie R, D, 1
12791 LOCUST, Will, Cherokee, NC, 47; 16259, Nellie, W, 46; Peter, S, 17; Tiney, D, 13
15788 LONG, Adam, Cherokee, NC, 50; 10044, Polly, W, 39; Lee-wih, S, 9; Nola, D, 7
15772 LONG, Charley, Cherokee, NC, 36; 10052, Sallie, W, 30 [?]; Long B, S, 9; Lucy, D, 7; Aggie, D, 5; Bettie, D, 3; Isaac, S, 1
 8653 LONG, Dobson, Robbinsville, NC, 44; John W, S, 10; Lizzie, D, 6; Wilson, S, 4
16268 LONG, Elsie, Cherokee, NC, 54
 6191 LONG, Jackson, Cherokee, NC, 55; Ella, D, 15
10035 LONG, Joe, Cherokee, NC, 47; 10036, Gah-we-li, S, 12
13039 LONG, John, Birdtown, NC, 35; 13040, Eve, W, 42
12991 LONG, Johnson, Birdtown, NC, 46; 12994, Maggie, W, 30
15793½ LONG, Lucy, Cherokee, NC, 76
34183 LONG, Maggie, Cherokee, NC, 13; Crow, Wesley S, Half-Bro, 4; By Amanda Smith, Gdn
16270 LONG, Peter, Cherokee, NC, 23
15708 LONG, Scott, Birdtown, NC, 52; 7735, Sallie, W, 50[?]; Lucy Ann, D, 16; Garlonuskie, S, 10; Emeline, D, 6; Da-gi-ni, D, 22
15817 LONG, Willie W, Wahhiyah, NC, 37
15901 LOSSEY, Solomon, Cherokee, NC, 7; By Henry Lossey, Gdn
34184 LOSSIE, Aggie, Whittier, NC, 27; Ross, McKinley, S, 5
15832 LOSSIE, John, Wahhiyah, NC, 46; 6195, Nancy, W, 52; Dobson, S, 19; Lloyd, S, 17
15685 LOSSIE, Nicer, Birdtown, NC, 27
 6202 LASSY, Leander, Cherokee, NC, 39; 6201, Annie, W, 25
 1443 LOUDERMILK, Cynthia, Culberson, NC, 45; Hollie, D, 16; Beckey, D, 7
 1446 LOUDERMILK, John, Culberson, NC, 25; Luther, S, 5; Rosey, D, 2

EASTERN CHEROKEES RESIDING EAST OF MISSISSIPPI RIVER.

KEY: Guion Miller Application Number; Name; Address; Relation (to Head); Age in 1906

3685 LOUDERMILK, Josephine, Culberson, NC, 33; Nora, D, 4; Elmer, S, 2; Cora, D, 1/12
2767 LOW, John J, Duluth, GA, 60
15866 LOWEN, John, Birdtown, NC, 9; By Judas Wesley, Gdn
12783 LOWEN, John, Cherokee, NC, 43; 12784, Sis, W, 46; Colonaheski, Katie, D of W, 18; Nanny, D of W, 9
16839 LOWEN, John B, Cherokee, NC, 46
22831 LUNSFORD, Daisy, Marble, NC, 18; Callie, D, 2

3194 McALISTER, Harriet C, Culberson, NC, 40
33529 McCLANAHAN, Ona, Tracy City, TN, 26; Nellie, D, 5; Earl, S, 2
26256 McCOY, David, Birdtown, NC, 33; Marinda, D, 6; James W, S, 5; Julia, D,3; Stella, D, 1
6197 McCOY, Eliza M, Birdtown, NC, 56
8146 McCOY, James D, Yucca, AL, 54; Stella May, D, 16; John T, S, 12
26257 McCOY, James M, Birdtown, NC, 26; William T, S, 1/6
26255 McCOY, John M, Birdtown, NC, 31; Pearson, S, 8; Mary, D, 5; James, S, 3; Bessie, D, 1; By John D McDaniel, Gdn
1792 McDANIEL, Lulie E, Madola, GA, 10
4174 McDONALD, Catherine, Ogreeta, NC, 83
18000 McDONALD, Mamie S, Dahlonega, GA, 30; Grace, D, 4; Ethel, D, 2
4175 McDONALD, Mary, Grape Creek, NC, 62; 5416, Harrison, S, 17; Belva, D, 19
2730 McDOUGAL, Samantha, Marblehill, GA, 32; Hershel, S, 9; Estes, D, 3; Lorene, D, 1

[McELREATH, Andrew See #20097] *(Note: entry separate from other family groups)*

20261 McELREATH, Charley, Hicks, GA, 25; Melley, D, 13; Jennie May, D, 7; Fred, S, 1
20100 McELREATH, Lewis W, Gainesville, GA,31; Floyd, S, 2; Flora, D, 1
20097 McELREATH, Andrew, Gainesville, GA, 23, RFD #5; India May, D, 1
4138 McLEMORE, Mary, Gainesville, GA, 31, RFD #5; Claud, S, 6; Frankie, S, 3; Fannie M, D, 1
20099 McELREATH, Mary A, Gainesville, GA, 65, RFD #5; Sarah C, D, 17
26106 McGEE, Sarah L, East Point, GA, 28
2924 McLEMORE, John W, Grape Creek, NC, 54; Esther Ann, D, 4; Cora May, D, 1
4138 McLEMORE, Mary, Lenoir City, TN, 40
2799 McLEMORE, Samuel H, Murphy, NC, 51; Morell M, S, 6; Samuel Ros, S, 1
29614 McLEMORE, William L, Lenoir City,TN,24; Dorothy, D, 3; Albert, S, 1/6; Emer, D, 9
95 McSPADDEN, Walter, Maryville, TN, 34, RFD #5; Faith H, D, 5

25856 MANEY, Cordela, Ocona Lufty, NC, 27; Flora B, D, 4; Minnie A, D, 2
13950 MARTIN, Daliskee, Birdtown, NC, 26; 33491, Angeline, W, 26; Su-da-yu, Sallie Ann, D of W, 2
24800 MARTIN, Essie, Cumming, GA, 25, RFD #1

EASTERN CHEROKEES RESIDING EAST OF MISSISSIPPI RIVER.

KEY: Guion Miller Application Number; Name; Address; Relation (to Head); Age in 1906

10633 MARTIN, Ester Janie, Gainesville, GA, 32, RFD #10; Van B, S, 15; David Lee, S, 14; Gurley S, 11; Frances, D, 10; Lenar, S, 7; Thomas E, S, 5; Kate, D, 3; Smith A, S, 1
15710 MARTIN, George, Birdtown, NC, 48; 6507, Lucy, W, 35; Wesley L, S, 13
20444 MARTIN, James G, Chattanooga, TN, 45, Cor 6th & Cross Sts
15711 MARTIN, Suate, Birdtown, NC, 60
13951 MARTIN, Thomas, Birdtown, NC, 21
21880 MARTIN, William W, Chattanooga, TN, 40, 115 Whiteside St
29411 MASHBURN, Harriett A, Murphy, NC, 28; Frank, S, 6; Bessie, D, 1; James L, S, 3; Sarah A, D, 1/3
30331 MASHBURN, Leora, Vest, NC, 23; Minnie, D, 5; Mattie, D, 3; Bertha, D, 1
25855 MATHEWS, Lillie, Ocona Lufty, NC, 25; Evie, D, 2
2893 MEADOWS, David T, Vayles, GA, 54
2890 MEADOWS, Elizabeth, Buren, GA, 80 [Died 8-12-1908]
26416 MEADOWS, John G, Vayles, GA, 21
2892 MEADOWS, Mary J, Buren, GA, 55

[MEE, Katie Vann See #21744] *(Note: entry separate from other family groups)*

36308 MERONEY, Bailey B, Murphy, NC, 25; Margaret A, D, 8; Richard B, S, 5; Felix P, S, 2
36309 MERONEY, Bessie, Murphy, NC, 25
36310 MERONEY, John S, Jr, Murphy, NC, 41; Lula, D, 15; Sallie B, D, 12; Mays, D, 9; Gertrude, D, 6; Bailey, S, 4; Della, D, 1; Fred, GS, 1
10336 MERONEY, Martha A, Murphy, NC, 70
36311 MERONEY, William H, Murphy, NC, 29
14960 MERRELL, Albert II, Chattanooga, TN, 31, 404 Ellen St
21765 MERRELL, John, Valhermoso Springs, AL, 40
21809 MERRELL, Ransey, Valhermoso Springs, AL, 38
18212 MICHAELS, Eliza, Norman, TN, 20
43887 MILLER, Carl, Spring Place, GA, 10, By Jas F Smith, Gdn
5375 MIMS, William P, Atlanta, GA, 42, 363 E Hunter, St; David Ross, S, 18; Robert A, S, 16; Ella M, D, 13; Cora L, D, 11; Margaret I, D, 4
3947 *NES-SEE, Mink*, Robbinsville, NC, 25 *(*NOTE: Could possibly be MINK, Nes-see)*
24801 MONDY, Maud, Cumming, GA, 23, RFD #1; Vera, D, 1
10997 MONROE, Nora A, Lenox, MA, 26
18198 MOON, Abner L, Norman, TN, 24
20376 MOON, Nellie, E Chattanooga, TN, 6; 20370, Benjamin, Bro, 10; 20371, Aaron, Bro, 13; 20374, Callie, Sis, 15; 20408, Thomas, Bro, 18 By Wm N Moon, Gdn
38880 MOOR, Cynthia A, Atlanta, GA, 25, RFD #6
22492 MOOR, Elizabeth B, Duluth, GA, 28
38879 MOOR, John Frederick, Atlanta, GA, 20, RFD #6
2851 MOOR, Sarah A, Atlanta, Ga, 58; Lottie, D, 18
3510 MOOR, Sarah L, Duluth, GA, 61
38878 MOOR, Wm Clifton, Atlanta, GA, 23, RFD #6

EASTERN CHEROKEES RESIDING EAST OF MISSISSIPPI RIVER.

KEY: Guion Miller Application Number; Name; Address; Relation (to Head); Age in 1906

35018 MOORE, Celia, Boaz, AL, 19; Malvin, S, ¼
2300 MORRISON, Ollie, Marble, NC, 26; Fred, S, 7; Jessie, D, 5; Beula, D, 1; Blanche, D, 1
11130 MUMBLEHEAD, John D, Almond, NC, 43; James B, S, 17; Rodgers L, S, 11; Charles C, S, 8; Rosey Bell, D, 2; Elizabeth, D, 1/12
19730 MURPHY, Arch, Nashville, TN, 47

[MURPHY, Jesse See 23891] *(Note: entry separate from other family groups)*

25275 MURPHY, Lillie Arch, Birdtown, NC, 1, By Mary Murphy, Gdn
23889 MURPHY, Mary, Birdtown, NC, 40; 23891, Jesse, Hus, 46; William, S, 16

15686 NED, Ezekiel, Birdtown, NC, 44; 15699, Annie, W, 44; Julie, D, 5
15900 NEGOOJAGE, Lidge W, Wahhiyah, NC, 53; James, S, 19; Ann Elizie, D, 17; Maggie, D, 11; Mark, S, 7; Ollie, D, 3

[NEQUAJACK, Davis W See #15847] *(Note: entry separate from other family groups)*

35895 NEWTON, Eva M, Sylvania, AL, 26; Bettie, D, 7; Pearl, D, 6; Lester, S, 4; John D, S, 2
3761 NEWTON, James, Chattanooga, TN, 34, 117 Lewis St; Eldrige, S, 6
2761 NICHOLS, Octavia N, Duluth, GA, 56
3737 NICHOLS, Taylor O, Dalton, GA, 35; Pryor O, S, 8
10040 NICK, Wesley C, Cherokee, NC, 65
12974 NIGAJACK, Lucinda, Folcroft, PA, 23
10051 NIGAJACK, Moses, Wahhiyah, NC, 21
10054 NIGAJACK, Nancy, Wahhiyah, NC, 40
10808 NOTTYTOM, Peter, Cherokee, NC, 37; 10809, Nancy, W, 22

2642 ODOM, Addie D, Dahlonega, GA, 28, RFD #3; Cicero, S, 3; Garland S, 1
2643 ODOM, Biddie D, Dahlonega, GA, 25; Loy Felton, S, 1

[OH-LEE-HEE-NEE See #2957] *(Note: entry separate from other family groups)*

16296 OKWATAGA, Elizabeth, Almond, NC, 67
4144 OLIVER, Lucinda, Hemlock, GA, 32; Ida, D, 3; Estie, D, 1
35452 OLIVER, Mary L, Collinsville, GL, 21, RFD #3; Beulah, D, 2
2431 O'NEAL, Eliza CE, Kosh, AL, 49; Conrad, S, 15; Beulah CE, 12; Wilburn K, S, 6
41550 O'NEAL, Laura, Bearden, TN, 42, RFD #1; Minnie M, D, 18; William EP, S, 15; Laura L, D, 11
16792 OO-CUMMA, Aleck, Cherokee, NC, 41
16803 OO-CUMMA, James, Cherokee, NC, 60[?]; 16290, Esther, W, 56; Enoch, S, 18; Annie, D, 12
39625 OO-CUMMA, Jennie, Cherokee, NC, 21
39624 OO-CUMMA, Wilson, Cherokee, NC, 29

EASTERN CHEROKEES RESIDING EAST OF MISSISSIPPI RIVER.

KEY: Guion Miller Application Number; Name; Address; Relation (to Head); Age in 1906

15814 OO-DAH-YIH, Cherokee, NC, 90
8655 OO-TAHL-KEE, Quakee, Robbinsville, NC, 76

[OSKIN-NEE See #2957]   *(Note: entry separate from other family groups)*

16794 OO-SOWIE, John, Cherokee, NC, 77; 16331, Jennie, W, 76; 16794, Willie, S, 19
16825 OO-SOWIE, Sam, Cherokee, NC, 46[?]; 12793, Susie, W, 27; 16825, Olise, D, 13; Nicie, D, 13; Paul, S, 6
39515 OO-SOWIE, Shell, Cherokee, NC, 33; 16257, Sallie, W, 34; Rachel, D, 9; Tahquette, D, 7; Olsinnih (Olsie), D, 2; Annie, D, 1
4226 OSKISON, John, Jr, New York City, NY, 32, 27 W 44th St; Helen Day, D, 1
11025 OTTER, Andrew, Birdtown, NC, 38; 8422, Sarah, W, 39; 11025, Lindia, D, 13; Jackson, S, 9; Matilda, D, 6; Ollick, S, 4; Elizabeth, D, 1
16820 OTTER, Nancy, Tomotla, NC, 25
16263 OTTER, Ollie, Judson, NC, 57
16265 OTTER, Wilson, Judson, NC, 21
16264 OTTER, Winnie, Almond, NC, 25; Sallie, D, 5
36132 OWL, Adam, Birdtown, NC, 45; 11149, Cornelia T, W, 52; 36132, Thomas, S, 19; Mose, S, 16; John, S, 14; Davis, S, 9; Samuel, S, 9; Martha, D, 6; Quincy, S, 1
16335 OWL, Allen, Cherokee, NC, 16, By Quety Owl, Gdn
6645 OWL, Blue, Whittier, NC, 50
11153 OWL, David, Cherokee, NC, 74
15794 OWL, James, Whittier, NC, 20
6216 OWL, John, Cherokee, NC, 45; Margaret, D, 3; Annie, D, 1/3
7740 OWL, Johnson, Wahhiyah, NC, 28; 26054, Stacy, W, 28
36153 OWL, Jonah, Cherokee, NC, 25
10050 OWL, Lloyd, Cherokee, NC, 33; Lula, D, 15; David, S, 13; George A, S, 12; Henry P, S, 9; Freal Mc, S, 7; Thomas WS, S, 1
6221 OWL, Sampson, Cherokee, NC, 52; Agner, AdD, 10
10056 OWL, So-kin-ni, Cherokee, NC, 17
24463 OWL, Solomon, Birdtown, NC, 42; Callie, D, 19; Dora, D, 16; Mark, S, 14; Jane, D, 12; Bryan, S, 9; Lloyd, S, 7; Cornelious, S, 4; Etha, D, 2
6206 OWL, Suate, Cherokee NC, 78; 6205, Dinah, W, 48; 6206, Amons, S, 16; William, S, 13; Enoch, S, 7; Betsy, D, 2
25650 OWL, Theodore, Birdtown, NC, 21
9986 OWL, William, Cherokee, NC, 22

21928 PADGETT, Isabella J, Chattanooga, TN, 41, 57 Lansing St; Mary M, D, 16; Ada C, D, 15; Artie W, S, 10; Nellie Dimma, D, 6
7476 PALMOUR, Myrtie K, Dawsonville, GA, 32, RFD #1
42 PANKEY, Elanora, Quarles, GA, 24; Dessie May, D, 3; Marvin, S, 1
15854 PANTHER, Bessie, Cherokee, NC, 53
39199 PANTHER, Job, Cherokee, NC, 22
16292 PANTHER, John, Cherokee, NC, 56; 15855, Nancy, W, 52
36326 PANTHER, Mark, Cherokee, NC, 29; 15785, Nancy, W, 23; 15785, Panther, Goliath, S, 5; Bradley, James, S of W, 1

EASTERN CHEROKEES RESIDING EAST OF MISSISSIPPI RIVER.

KEY: Guion Miller Application Number; Name; Address; Relation (to Head); Age in 1906

2626 PARKER, Caroline, Dalton, GA, 52, #8 Pine St; Aaron, S, 16
20502 PARKER, Josie, Chattanooga, TN, 30; #8 Long St
27216 PARKER, Julian, Rome, GA, 35; Paul, S, 1
11002 PARRIS, Catharine, Culverson, NC, 23; Laura May, D, 1/12
12993 PARTRIDGE, Mose, Birdtown, NC, 23; 28782, Sallie, W, 19
12995 PARTRIDGE, Nelly, Birdtown, NC, 53
12992 PARTRIDGE, Winnie E, Trough, SC, 20
7676 PASCHAL, Geo Walter, Washington, DC, 65, 1918 Calvert St
22684 PASCHAL, Walter, Washington, DC, 25, 1918 Calvert St
12778 PASSMORE, Nancy J, Lookout, NC, 29; Thomas, S, 5; AL, D, 4; Cardie, D, 2
803 PATTERSON, Ella, Dora, GA, 30; Onzo, S, 10; Ethel, D, 8; Elizabeth, D, 6; Celie, D, 5; Hobert, S, 3; Arvis, D, 1/6
1260 PATTERSON, Lula, Culverson, NC, 28; Olden, S, 5; Elmer, S, 1
3317 PAYNE, David L, Tellico Plains, TN, 32; Duke, S, 8; Ada, D, 6
12101 PAYNE, Elisha, Nina, NC, 25
22493 PAYNE, Emma OL, Duluth, GA, 24; Louise, D, 1/6
745 PAYNE, Felix, Danielsville, GA, 39, RFD #4; Sally, D, 16; Betty, D, 14; Hazel, D, 12; Mack, S, 10; Lucy, D, 7; Ephraim, S, 4; Ellen, D, 2
27867 PAYNE, James M, Letitia, NC, 30; Rollen T, S, 9; Albert F, S, 7; Grace L, D, 3
12099 PAYNE, Jim, Nina, NC, 19
12108 PAYNE, John, Nina, NC, 15
12107 PAYNE, Mary Jane, Unaka, NC, 28
2690 PAYNE, Thomas, Letitia, NC, 62; Oliver, S, 14
29150 PAYNE, William E, Letitia, NC, 34; Polly E, D, 10; William A S, 3; Lydia M, D, ¼

[PENDLETON, Walter See #14712] *(Note: entry separate from other family groups)*

31219 PERKINS, Georgia, Rossville, GA, 26; Burt, S, 5; Gordon, S, 3
23429 PERRY, George M, Tate, GA, 22; 1696, PERRY, Julia D, Tate, GA, 43; Watson, S, 14; Mamie, D, 10; Julia B, D, 6; William C, S, 3
15813 PHEASANT, Cherokee, NC, 99
12762 PHEASANT, John, Wahhiyah, NC, 56; 10034, Waggie, W, 53; Dora, D, 16
39200 PHEASANT, William, Swain, NC, 24
23428 PINSON, Eula, Dawsonville, GA, 24; Clara, D, 7; Guy, S, 5; Bertha, D, 2
23116 POPE, James, Hemp, GA, 29
1372 POPE, Martha, Hemp, GA, 52; Lizzie L, D, 16; Elisia L, D, 13
23115 POPE, Mary H, Hemp, GA, 26
23114 POPE, Thomas L, Hemp, GA, 31; Allie T, D, 10; Blaine, S, 5; Maybell, D, 8; Harley, S, 2
23117 POPE, William FL, Hemp, GA, 34; Allen, S, 7; Aora, D, 4
35556 PORTER, Florence S, Franklin, NC, 43; James D, S, 17; Iris, D, 15

[PORTER, Tommy See #11155] *(Note: entry separate from other family groups)*

EASTERN CHEROKEES RESIDING EAST OF MISSISSIPPI RIVER.

KEY: Guion Miller Application Number; Name; Address; Relation (to Head); Age in 1906

36202 POWELL, Doogah, Wahhiyah, NC, 38; Mose, S, 19; Stansell, S, 17; Sarah, D, 7; Holmes, S, 5; Winnie, D, 3
9940 POWELL, James E, Atlanta, GA, 35, 137 Park Ave; Frank E, S, 9; Vernon, S, 7; Sadie, D, 5
6194 POWELL, John A, Marble, NC, 53
9941 POWELL, John C, Morganton, GA, 34; Gober, S, 5
15049 POWELL, Moses, Wahhiyah, NC, 18
15831 POWELL, Stancel, Wahhiyah, NC, 16; Sarah, Sis, 8; Holmes, Bro, 3; Winnie, Sis, 1; By Took Powell, Gdn
118 POWELL, William, Blue Ridge, GA, 47
28114 PULLIUM, Caroline, Andrews, NC, 26; Galusha, S, 7; Elizabeth, D, 5; Decatur, S, 3
18325 PURYEAR, Frank M, Villanow, GA, 18, RFD #1; Hamp Y, Bro, 13; Mary, A, Sis, 10; By Hamp Y Puryear, Gdn

15693 QUAIN, Wodesutta, Birdtown, NC, 42; Walter, S, 2
2435 QUARLES, Henry B, Tailscreek, GA, 30; Charley, S, 6; Luther, S, 3
40 QUARLES, James D, Quarles, GA, 34; Mary B, D, 14; Rosy B, D, 7; Henry G, S, 1
3022 QUARLES, Mary A, Quarles, GA, 54; Roxie A, D, 17; Bearl G, S, 3
15776 QUEEN, Jasper, Cherokee, NC, 14; By Simpson Queen, Gdn
42917 QUEEN, Levi, Whittier, NC, 36; 15812, Mary, W, 26; Mindy, D, 12; Abraham, S, 8; Etta, D, 5; Malinda, D, 3
15804 QUEEN, Lucindy, Loco Creek, NC, 59; Taylor, Jimmy, GS, 3
42920 QUEEN, Simpson, Whittier, NC, 36; 42918, Sallie, W, 26; Ollie, D, 7; Nolie, D, 5; Mary, D, 3; Bessie, D, 1

[RACKLEY---See RATLIFF]   *(Note: entry separate from other family groups)*

25955 RAINEY, Janie, Cottage Grove, TN, 28; Homer, S, 4; Annie Catherine, D, 1
1411 RALSTON, Violet, Dalton, GA, 15; Lucy, Sis, 11; Luke, Bro, 9
6553 RANDOLPH, Letitia ML, Marietta, GA, 33, 827 Whitlock Ave
2232 RAPER, Alexander, Culberson, NC, 61; 4537, Iowa, D, 18
4534 RAPER, Charles B, Culberson, NC, 33; Denver Lee, S, 8; Deltia C, D, 6; Pearl, D, 1; Emory, S, 1/8
31961 RAPER, Elizie, Christopher, GA, 11; By Theodoosia Raper, Gdn
25749 RAPER, Gano, Andrews, NC, 23
18592 RAPER, Henry C, Ducktown, TN, 38; James C, S, 13; Miran G, S, 10; Claud H, S, 3; Maudy Lu, D, ½
335 RAPER, Jackson, Farner, TN, 37; Homer, S, 5; Mary, D, 3; Manda, D, 1
3765 RAPER, Jackson, Rossville, GA, 60
23519 RAPER, James, Euchee, TN, 34, RFD #2; William N, S, 11; Gracie, D, 9; James, Jr, S, 3; George W, S, 7; Clay, S, 5
2110 RAPER, James B, Ivy Log, GA, 41; Elisha, S, 18; Georgia Ann, D, 16; Alvin, S, 14; Lon, S, 12; Ivy Ann, D, 10; Delia, D, 8; Mary, D, 7; Dovie, D, 5; Dessie, D, 3
10999 RAPER, James T, Isabella, TN, 30; Harvey L S, 5; Harley T, S, 3

EASTERN CHEROKEES RESIDING EAST OF MISSISSIPPI RIVER.

KEY: Guion Miller Application Number; Name; Address; Relation (to Head); Age in 1906

 4532 RAPER, Jesse Lafayette, Culberson, NC, 37; Cli, S, 8; Claude, S, 7; Jerley, S, 5
26007 RAPER, John H, Rossville, GA, 33; Lillie May, D, 1
 4533 RAPER, John Henry, Culberson, NC, 27; Viola, D, 4; Iven, S, 2
32228 RAPER, Lou, Murphy, NC, 25
 3988 RAPER, Margaret G, Highland Park Sta, TN, 14 Rt 1, RFD, By Tennessee Dillard, Gdn
 4535 RAPER, Marshal, Culberson, NC, 35; Marty, S, 14; Effie, D, 12; Alven, S, 8; Clinton, S, 4; Ever, D, 2
  381 RAPER, Nathan, Euchee, TN, 55, RFD #2; Sam, S, 20; Willie, S, 18; Mamie, D, 16; Naomie, D, 13
  237 RAPER, Thomas W, Murphy, NC, 50; James, S, 10; Martin, S, 17; Lizzie, D, 8; Julia, D, 6; Clifton, S, 1; Whoote, S, 19
26008 RAPER, William, Rossville, GA, 19
32229 RAPER, William B, Murphy, NC, 26
 4539 RAPER, William T, Culberson, NC, 39; Jessie, D, 15; Edger, S, 12; Verdy, D, 10; Dathney, D, 8; Guss, S, 4; Girley, D, 2
 8428 RATLEY, Jim, Cherokee, NC, 60
11140 RATLEY, Lucy, Cherokee, NC, 62
12771 RATLIFF, Loyd, Birdtown, NC, 30
12772 RATLIFF, William, Birdtown, NC, 33; 27172, Lizzie, W, 28; Emma, D, 5; Jacob, S, 2
 8661 RATTLER, George, Robbinsville, NC, 34; Abie, S, 13; Alucy, D, 12; Rachel, D, 9; Henson, S, 7; Morgan, S, 4; Minda, D, 2
15698 RATTLER, Jesse, Tomotla, NC, 27
 6413 RATTLER, John, Tomotla, NC, 21
 6417 RATTLER, Nancy, Tomotla, NC, 50; Jason, S, 17
26240 RATTLER, Polly, Robbinsville, NC, 30; Alice, D, 13; Lucy, D, 12; Rachel, D, 10; Henson, S, 8; Morgan, S, 6
33655 RAY, Alexander W, Birmingham, AL, 24, 4037 5th Ave; Grace Gertrude, D, 3; Vernon Dean, S, 2
14216 RAY, John N, Avondale, AL, 43, 4024 1st Ave, N; RD, S, 20; John F, S, 7; Fred J, S, 11; Charles R, S, 10; Alex W, S, 5

[RAY, Lula Ella & family See 4778]   *(Note: entry separate from other family groups)*

14217 RAY, Robert B, Birmingham, AL, 40, 2321-½ 2nd Ave, N
14215 RAY, William, Cleveland, TN, 23
11791 REDFEARN, Martha, Saulsbury, TN, 28; John Earl, S, 5; Jesse Dewitt, S, 2
12787 REED, Dave, Robbinsville, NC, 46
12280 REED, Fidille, Halifax, NC, 32, C/o Supt State Farm
16258 REED, Jesse, Cherokee, NC, 58; 16252, Maggie, W, 56
16266 REED, Lucy Ann, Judson, NC, 30
 6630 REED, Rachel, Cherokee, NC, 55
 2775 REED, Susan J, Chattanooga, TN, 36
16808 REID, Adam, Cherokee, NC, 30; 16829, Rachel, W, 21; Johnson, S, 4
16797 REID, Duweese, Cherokee, NC, 24; 39626, Nannie, W, 24

EASTERN CHEROKEES RESIDING EAST OF MISSISSIPPI RIVER.

KEY: Guion Miller Application Number; Name; Address; Relation (to Head); Age in 1906

16260 REID, James, Cherokee, NC: 50
16261 REID, Peter, Cherokee, NC, 56; 16831, Jimmie, S, 16; Lloyd, GS, 16; Cindy, GD, 10
16795 REID, Willie, Cherokee, NC: 25 [?]; 16256, Irene, W, 33; Noah, S, 11; Spade, S, 8; Winnie, D, 1/6
34956 RICE, Fannie, Pink, AL, 14
27690 RICHARD, Mamie, Letitia, NC, 19
12177 RING, Charles H, Macon, GA, 35
12175 RING, Ella N, Macon, GA, 35
12176 RING, George W, Macon, GA, 38
 1863 ROBERSON, Edward C, Culberson, NC, 29; Charley H, S, 2
10350 ROBERSON, Eleanor, Adairsville, GA, 56; Sarah, D, 19; Ginty, S, 2
 4540 ROBERSON, Ellen, Culberson, NC, 43; Fannie, D, 12; Emaline, D, 10; Haddley, S, 7
 1862 ROBERSON, Gita, Culberson, NC, 15; By James R Roberson, Gdn
 2472 ROBERSON, Mary, Suit, NC, 32
 2473 ROBERSON, Willis O, Culberson, NC, 26
19791 ROBERTS, Charlotte, Apalachia, NC, 23; Walter, S, 4; Fred, S, 2; 44802, Smith, Callie, D, 5; By Leander Murphy, Gdn
 1861 ROBERTSON, Thomas, Peachtree, NC, 23; William, S, 3

[ROBIN, Richard See #7733]   *(Note: entry separate from other family groups)*

 3759 ROBINSON, Birgie, Chattanooga, TN, 24, 614 Cowart St; Charles, S, 13; Willie, S, 6
34456 RODDY, Elbert D, Ooltewah, TN, 30; Jessie R, D, 9; Leta M, D, 6; Ralph, S, 4
17342 RODGERS, Cordelia, Cherokee, NC, 30 [?]
 1860 RODGERS, Martha C, Culberson, NC, 37; George E, S, 15
  400 ROGERS, Augustus L, Duluth, GA, 57; Ruth A, D, 14; James C, S, 11; Robert C, S, 11
23698 ROGERS, Clio A, Duluth, GA, 25
23697 ROGERS, Ernest H, Duluth, GA, 20
 3502 ROGERS, Florence S, Menlo, GA, 51
 2519 ROGERS, Jeanette, Culberson, NC, 60
27774 ROGERS, John W, Duluth, GA, 23
23699 ROGERS, Julia EM Duluth, GA, 33
27775 ROGERS, Louise E, Duluth, GA, 20
 1793 ROGERS, Pearlie Ann, Cherry Log, GA, 20
29627 ROGERS, Raymond C, Marietta, GA, 31; Robert C, S, 5; Howard W, S, 4; Ernest P, S, 2; Elizabeth, D, 5/12
 3262 ROGERS, Robert N, Duluth, GA, 68
 6650 ROGERS, William, Ivy Log GA, 41; Boney, S, 14; Osker, S, 10; Viller, S, 7; Floid, S, 4; Aster, D, 1
 3764 ROLLINGS, Dovie, Chattanooga, TN, 47, 109 W Lewis St
  730 ROPETWISTER, John, Robbinsville, NC, 55; 6765, Annie or Arneach, W, 60

EASTERN CHEROKEES RESIDING EAST OF MISSISSIPPI RIVER.

KEY: Guion Miller Application Number; Name; Address; Relation (to Head); Age in 1906

30100 ROSE, Florence, Cheoah, NC, 33; Bonnie, D, 14; Buffalo Bill, S, 13; Jake, S, 12; Gracie, D, 8; Nora, D, 4; Carlie, S, 2
3844 ROSE, Ida, Ocoee, TN, 28; Myrtle, D, 8; Jennings, S, 4; Annie, D, 3; Freeman, S, 1; Leslie, S, ¼
15902 ROSE, Adam, Wahhiyah, NC, 24; 41787, Mandy, W, 18; Rachel, D, 1
14247 ROSS, Cain, Wahhiyah, NC, 19
15904 ROSS, James, Cherokee, NC, 58; 15715, Rosa, W, 66; 15903, William, S, 17
4778 RAY, Lula Ella, Tolona, GA, 24; Charles, S, 3; William, S, 1/12
5483 RUDDLES, Irena, Murphy, NC, 80

3961 SAKE, Che-wah-nee, Robbinsville, NC, 66
2937 SAKE, Nellie, Robbinsville, NC, 56

[SA-LA-LU-SI, Susannah See 316023] *(Note: entry separate from other family groups)*

10057 SALOLANEETA, Bird, Cherokee, NC, 63; 10053, Lucy, W, 53
7735 SALOLANEETA, Henry, Cherokee, NC, 36; 7737, Aggie, W, 28
10029 SALOLANEETA, John, Cherokee, NC, 60[?]
10030 SALOLANEETA, John, Jr, Cherokee,NC,38; 10047, Laura, W, 40; 10030, Lizzie, D, 13; John, S, 9; Jessie J, D, 1; 10047, Sawnooka, Margaret, D of W, 20; Crow, Nonie, D of W, 17
6217 SALOLANEETA, Jonas, Birdtown, NC, 33
10031 SALOLANEETA, Lindy, Cherokee, NC, 44
15774 SAMPSON, James, Cherokee, NC, 51; 15769, Sallie, W, 50
17185 SANDERS, Polly, Cherokee, NC, 47; Listy, S, 18; Julia, D, 15; Mose, S, 10
3023 SANFORD, Sarah M, Quarles, GA, 32; William D, S, 14; Emily M, D, 11; Andrew H, S, 9; George H, S, 7; John H, S, 5; James H, S, 2
1536 SATTERFIELD Amanda E, Hedwig, GA, 24; Henry T, S, 2
5244 SATTERFIELD, Brilla D, Dahlonega, GA, 49
11141 SAWNOOKA, Adam, Cherokee, NC, 20
12975 SAWNOOKA, Jackson, Cherokee, NC, 24
15899 SAWNOOKA, James, Cherokee, NC, 18
12790 SAWNOOKA, John, Whittier, NC, 51, RFD, #1
11135 SAWNOOKA, John, Jr, Cherokee, NC, 45; 6225, Margaret, W, 43; Jenny, D, 3; 6033, Trottingwolf, Ned, S of W, 17
12785 SAWNOOKA, Joseph, Cherokee, NC, 34
12796 SAWNOOKA, Josephine, Cherokee, NC, 14
42162 SAWNOOKA, Malinda, Cherokee, NC, 20

[SAWNOOKA, Margaret See #10047] *(Note: entry separate from other family groups)*

6654 SAWNOOKA, Nancy, Cherokee, NC, 55
12754 SAWNOOKA, Nancy, Whittier, NC, 30
28751 SAWNOOKA, Nannie, Folcroft, PA, 30

[SAWNOOKA, Ollie See #39196] *(Note: entry separate from other family groups)*

EASTERN CHEROKEES RESIDING EAST OF MISSISSIPPI RIVER.

KEY: Guion Miller Application Number; Name; Address; Relation (to Head); Age in 1906

11119 SAWNOOKA, Polk, Cherokee, NC, 32; Nanny, D, 9; Wal-lin-ny, D, 1
16889 SAWNOOKA, Rachel, Carlisle, PA, 19
15905 SAWNOOKA, Sallie, Cherokee, NC, 18
12163 SAWNOOKA, Samuel, Altoona, PA, 28
10068 SAWNOOKA, Soggy, Cherokee, NC, 14; Sallie, Sis, 8; By Lydia Jessannih, Gdn
7748 SAWNOOKA, Stilwell, Cherokee, NC, 60; 10061, Stacy, W, 48; 7749, Windy, S, 18; Thompson, S, 16; Amineeta, D, 12; Cindy, D, 7; Savannah, D, 2
12788 SAWNOOKA, Stilwell, Whittier, NC, 15; By John Sawnooka, Gdn
12786 SAWNOOKA, William, Cherokee, NC, 36; Stephen E,S, 6; Osley B, S, 1; Joseph A, S, 3
10032 SAWYER, Kiyini, Cherokee, NC, 34; Thomas, S, 1
11125 SCOTT, Camble, Wahhiyah, N, 40
7743 SCREAMER, Enos, Wahhiyah, NC, 40
16272 SCREAMER, James, Cherokee, NC, 47; 11133, Cinda, W, 37; 16272, Cain, S, 6; 16272, Soggy, S, 3
12973 SCREAMER, Manus, Cherokee, NC, 24
1535 SEITZ, Georgia A, Burtsboro, GA, 23
1534 SEITZ, Jenny Linn, Burtsboro, GA, 48; Henry G, S, 19; Jenny L, D, 14
1533 SEITZ, John C, Burtsboro, GA, 21
7738 SEQUOYAH, Wahhiyah, NC, 68[?]
15857 SEQUOYAH, Jackalia, Wahhiyah, NC, 48; 15858, Louisa, W, 47; 15857, Tahquitte, S, 17; Richard, S, 9; 15858, Amanda, D, 8; Suannah, D, 5; Alice, D, 3
19804 SEQUOYAH, Lizzie, Cherokee, NC, 14
18052 SEQUOYAH, Luzena, Wahhiyah, NC, 25
19291 SEQUOYAH, Noah, Wahhiyah, NC, 22
15827 SEQUOYAH, RunningWolf,Swayney,NC,28; 10055, Wolfe, Mollie, W, 26; Lloyd, S, 7; Emmaneatte, D, 5; Thomas, S, 3; Jinsey, D, 1
336 SHADWICK, Alice, Farner, TN, 37; Manuel H, S, 16; Mary L, D, 14; Clair, S, 12; Erven, S, 9; Ensola, S, 5; Eddie Lonzo, S, 2
28850 SHASTEEN, James W, Winchester, TN, 28
12374 SHASTEEN, Mary, Winchester, TN, 59; Eliza E, D, 20; Nannie B, D, 17
28852 SHASTEEN, Richmond S, Jr, Decherd, TN, 29
28851 SHASTEEN, Sofrona E, Winchester, TN, 25
29006 SHASTEEN, Thomas F, Winchester, TN, 35; Roy H, S, 6
24923 SHASTEEN, William B, Winchester, TN, 34; Lyman Lee, S, 2; Virginia E, D, 1
25436 SHED, Martha JR, Dougherty, GA, 29; Harley R, S, 3; James G, S, 2

[SHELL, Andy See #15787] *(Note: entry separate from other family groups)*

8769 SHELL, John, Cherokee, NC, 54; 11147, Sally, W, 48; Hetty Feather, D, 9
11148 SHELL, Ute, Cherokee, NC, 29; 11146, Mattie, W, 20; 11148, Joe, S, 5; Bessie, D, 3; Alice, D, 1
9784 SHERRILL, John Ute, Cherokee, NC, 36; 9782, Mollie, W, 28; 9784, Kinny, S, 7; Solomon, S, 5; Julia, D, 1/6
15183 SILVER, Emma, Blaine, GA, 32; Emma, D, 12; Grady, S, 7; Edgar, S, 4; Victor, S, 2

EASTERN CHEROKEES RESIDING EAST OF MISSISSIPPI RIVER.

KEY: Guion Miller Application Number; Name; Address; Relation (to Head); Age in 1906

  602 SITTON, Emma, Dawsonville, GA, 50
  556 SIVLEY, Crocia Ann, Valdeau, TN, 48; Claudie B, D, 19; Joseph, S, 17; Caroline, D, 14; May, D, 11; Roy, S, 9
23172 SIVLEY, Jas D, Valdeau, TN, 20
17465 SIXKILLER, Jesse Martin, Madison, IL, 11; By Laura Malicoate, Gdn

[SKEE-KEE, Jess See #11151]   (Note: entry separate from other family groups)

22363 SKELLEY, Cora Belle, Morrison, IL, 35; Charles, S, 15; Joseph, S, 14
  626 SKITTY, Severe, Cherokee, NC, 58

[SMITH, Callie See #44802]   (Note: entry separate from other family groups)

29680 SMITH, Carrie, Rockmart, GA, 27; George, S, 7; Dell, D, 4; Evelyn, D, 2
 4182 SMITH, Charley, Walland TN, 43; Emma C, D, 19; Henry H, S, 17
 2366 SMITH, Cicero K, Marietta, GA, 32; Mamie, D, 3; Eula, D, 1/6 [Died 4-23-1907]
 5484 SMITH, Daliah or Delilah, Murphy, NC, 36; Emma, D, 16; Sylena, D, 12; Marshall, S, 9; Lizzie, D, 4
34193 SMITH, Duffie, Cherokee, NC, 26
26840 SMITH, Erskine Irene, Nolensville, TN, 21
34192 SMITH, Frances E, Cherokee, NC, 20
11706 SMITH, George L, Tellico Plains, TN, 25
 6192 SMITH, Henry, Cherokee, NC, 57; Russell, S, 2
12767 SMITH, Jacob, Cherokee, NC, 27; 16275, Olive Larch, W, 27
34191 SMITH, James D, Cherokee, NC, 28
 1516 SMITH, John, Madola, GA, 53; Ellick, S, 24 [Unsound mind]; Charlie, S, 20; Arizona, D, 18; Fanzy, D, 16; Minnie, D, 13; Viola, D, 11; Beulah, D, 9; Bessie, D, 7
 9820 SMITH, John Henry, McCays, TN, 23; Stella, D, 1/6
 2689 SMITH, John Q, Nina, NC, 36; James, S, 13; Josephine, D, 11; Rosy, D, 9; Bessie, D, 5; Robert, S, 2
10342 SMITH, Lewis H, Robbinsville, NC, 62; 3951, Nancy, W, 56
10346 SMITH, Lorella, Brentwood, TN, 53; Addie Lela, D, 18; Wallace J, S, 16; Clea N, D,13
15704 SMITH, Lloyd, Cherokee, NC, 33; Robson, S, 7; Elizabeth, D, 5; Noah, S, 4; Teney, S, 2; Etta, D, 19; Crow, Wesley, S, 17; Smith, Jessie, D, 14; Mandie, D, 11; Martha, D, 10
 6193 SMITH, Mark T, Cherokee, NC, 53; Charity, D, 17; Oliver, S, 10
 6557 SMITH, Martha, Walland, TN, 71
38719 SMITH, Missouri, Helitrope, TN, 30, [Died 8-14-1906 by husband]; Willie May B, D, 6; James Harris, S, 4; Calvin, S, 2
40616 SMITH, Noah, Cherokee, NC, 23
 2817 SMITH, Ross B, Nina, NC, 66; 2471, Cynthia, W, 54
11605 SMITH, Roxie, Cherokee, NC, 24
 7477 SMITH, Sallie A, Atlanta, GA, 44, 356 Woodward Ave; Mabel, D, 17; Robert E, S, 15; Winnie, D, 13

EASTERN CHEROKEES RESIDING EAST OF MISSISSIPPI RIVER.

KEY: Guion Miller Application Number; Name; Address; Relation (to Head); Age in 1906

- **18555** SMITH, Samuel E, Bigspring, TN, 33; Edgar, S,11; Myrtle, D, 7; Nellie, D, 5; Earl, S, 3; John C, S, 1
- **2025** SMITH, Sylvester A, Blue Ridge, GA, 49
- **7739** SMITH, Thaddeus S, Cherokee, NC, 28; Hartman, S, 9; Mary, D, 7; Gerald, S, 3; Gracie, D, 1
- **12768** SMITH, Thomas, Cherokee, NC, 22
- **26841** SMITH, Willie Clark, Nolensville, TN, 27
- **3958** SMOKER, John, Robbinsville, NC, 41; 3957, Maggie, W, 35; 3958, Cindy, D, 18; Jim, S, 16; Will, S, 9; Peter, S, 5; Charley, S, 2
- **16840** SMOKER, Lloyd, Judson, NC, 34; 15298, Ahyoster, W, 54
- **3061** SMOKER, Will, Robbinsville, NC, 38; 2957, Os-kin-nee, W, 27; 3061, Smoker, Kwous, S, 10; Awie, D, 8; Ganeleck, S, 5; Lizzie, D, 2
- **16832** SMOKER, Axe Sam, Robbinsville, NC,24; 3952, Stacy, W, 22; Bascom, S, 4; Olive, D, 1
- **9781** SNEED, John Harris, Cherokee, NC, 59; Campbell, S, 19
- **34190** SNEED, Manco, Cherokee, NC, 20
- **27429** SNEED, Osco, Cherokee, NC, 27
- **10069** SNEED, Samuel, Cherokee, NC, 49; Mary, D, 11; Annie, D, 9; Maud, D, 7
- **24400** SNEED, Veco, Birdtown, NC, 30; Sarah, D, 4; SB, S, 2
- **2469** SNEED, William S, Nina, NC, 44
- **809** SNYDER, Susannah, Sweden, GA, 62

[SOL-EE-OL-EE-SEE, Waddie See #15828] *(Note: entry separate from other family groups)*

[SOLOLANEETA, Annie See #6201]
[SOLOLANEETA, Leander See #6202] *(Note: entries separate from other family groups)*

[SOLOLANEETA See SALOLANEETA]

[SOUNOOKE See SAWNOOKA]

- **800** SOWTHER, Dora, Dora, GA, 18
- **2731** SPARKS, Sarah A, Dahlonega, GA, 34; Belle, D, 14; Carl, S, 9; Harlie, S, 7; Leroy, S, 5
- **13036** SQUIRREL, David, Birdtown, NC, 32; 29398, Nancy, W, 31; 13036, Kimsey, S, 10; Norah, D, 8; Dinah, D, 6; Daniel, S, 4; Ollie, D, 1
- **10074** SQUIRREL, Fox, Cherokee, NC, 46
- **13037** SQUIRREL, George, Birdtown, NC, 40; 32045, Quattie, W, 36; Awee, S, 17; Sarah, D, 13; Nora, D, 11; Sequtteh, D, 9; Mary, D, 7; Nancy, D, 6
- **6639** STALLCUP, Nancy, Marble, NC, 46
- **18497** STAMEY, Winnie A, Madisonvile, TN, 24; Pearley, D, 4; James, S, 2; Arch, S, 1
- **11108** STANDINGDEER, Andy, Cherokee, NC, 54; 6208, Margaret, W, 50
- **10025** STANDINGDEER, Carl W,Cherokee,NC,25; 12765, Mary S, W, 33
- **16804** STANDINGDEER, Caroline, Cherokee, NC, 18
- **2003** STANDINGDEER, Junaluska, Cherokee, NC, 25
- **6207** STANDINGDEER, Lowin, Cherokee, NC, 21

EASTERN CHEROKEES RESIDING EAST OF MISSISSIPPI RIVER.

KEY: Guion Miller Application Number; Name; Address; Relation (to Head); Age in 1906

16826 STANDINGDEER, Margrette, Cherokee, NC, 46
10037 STANDINGDEER, Nancy, Cherokee, NC, 58
12763 STANDINGDEER, Wesley, Cherokee, NC 52; 10060, Nana, W, 50
12751 STANDINGWATER, Aleck, Cherokee NC, 50; 12759, Elsinnah, D, 12
17774 STANTON, Florence, Chattanooga, TN, 29, 223 Elizabeth St
24725 STEWART, Cordelia W, Green Brier, TN, 30; Arthur T, S, 13; Levi, S, 11; Dora, D, 7; Lucinda, D, 6
27691 STILES, Mary, Letitia, NC, 37; Minnie, D, 16; Gilbert, S, 13; Emy, D, 11; Oliver, S, 8; Clem, S, 3; Hal, S, ¼
27689 STILES, Theodosia E, Kinsey, NC, 28; Thomas Luster, S, 9; Virgil, D(?), 6; Alma, D, 4; Floyd, S, 1

[STONER, Willie E See #7520]
[STONER, Thelma T, See #7520]   *(Note: entries separate from other family groups)*

5457 STRICKLAND, Mary F, Cumming, GA, 39; Roy, S, 12; Ellene, D, 8; John Robert, S, 6; Clifford A, S, 1
32335 STULL, Missouri, Lexington, KY, 48, 568 E 3rd St
15711 SUATE, Martin, Birdtown, NC, 60

[SU-DA-YU, Sallie Ann See #33491]   *(Note: entry separate from other family groups)*

26773 SULLINS, Paul S, White, GA, 22
28360 SUMMEROUR, Junia E, Albertville, AL, 30; Florence, D, 12; Katherine, D, 9; Milton, S, 7; Sam, S, 5; Ethel, D, 2
6212 SUTEGI, Cherokee, NC, 69; 12775, Mary, W, 55
24746 SUTER, Louvenia W, Green Brier, TN, 35; Charles W, S, 17; John Riley, S, 16
24726 SUTER, Martha, Adams, TN, 33; Maggie, D, 15; Mary, D, 14; George, S, 10; Lueller, D, 7; Diller, S, 4
26405 SUTTON, Nancy, Plainsville, GA, 21
11132 SUWAGGIE, Wadasutta, Wahhiyah, NC, 61; 11131, Wadasutta, Anna, W, 43
26890 SWAYNEY, Arizona, Wahhiyah, NC, 31
26891 SWAYNEY, John W, Wahhiyah, NC, 23
7741 SWAYNEY, Laura, Swayney, NC, 49; Jesse, S, 18; Calle, S, 14; Luzane, D, 8
27655 SWAYNEY, Lorenzo D, Bigcove, NC, 27; Amanda, D, 5; Frank, S, 1
36000 SWIFT, Benjamin W, Chicago, IL, 38; Frank B, S, 9; Mabel, D, 6
15907 SWIMMER, Lucian, Cherokee, NC, 22
43886 SWIMMER, Runaway, Swayney, NC, 29; 10021, Annie, W, 25; Littlejohn, Mary, D of W, 14
10774 SWIMMER, Tom, Wahhiyah, NC, 43

12789 TAHQUETTE, John A, Cherokee, NC, 36; 10043, Annie E, W, 32; Emily, D, 2/3
3950 TAH-QUIT, Martha, Robbinsville, NC, 45

[TAH-TAH-YEH See #15785]   *(Note: entry separate from other family groups)*

EASTERN CHEROKEES RESIDING EAST OF MISSISSIPPI RIVER.

KEY: Guion Miller Application Number; Name; Address; Relation (to Head); Age in 1906

6222 TAIL, Jim, Cherokee, NC, 60[?]
9242 TA-LA-LA-, John, Birdtown, NC, 57; 16301, Rebecca, W, 56; French, Ross, GS, 4
9241 TA-LA-LA, Will, Birdtown, NC, 66; 16302, Lucy, W, 46; Thomas, S, 17; Jackson, S, 14; McKinley, S, 6;
12797 TATHAM, Stella, Bryson City, NC, 25; Olive, D, 2
16337 TAYLOR, Jack, Birdtown, NC, 16; John, Bro, 14; Bessie, Sis, 16; Oo-la-i-way, Bro, 8; Temsey, Sis, 6; David, Bro, 3; By Sallie Lambert, Gdn
12792 TAYLOR, Jesse, Birdtown, NC, 41; 16837, Stacy, W, 46
15690 TAYLOR, John, Birdtown, NC, 73; 15688, Sallie, W, 60
16807 TAYLOR, John, Cherokee, NC, 47
39623 TAYLOR, Julius, Cherokee, NC, 28; 16289, Stacy, W, 30
16336 TAYLOR, Liza, Birdtown, NC, 43
42914 TAYLOR, Olkinney, Cherokee, NC, 22
42916 TAYLOR, Sherman, Cherokee, NC, 24; 42915, Maggie, W, 18; Olkinny, S, 2
15801 TAYLOR, Rachel, Birdtown, NC, 38
17707 TAYLOR, Thomas E, Vests, NC, 28
9907 TUATLAY, Nancy, Robbinsville, NC, 77
3953 TEE-CEE-TES-KEE, Sallie, Robbinsville, NC, 41; Jessie, D, 19; Arach, S, 9; Arowee, D, 6; Jonah, S, 3
13253 TE-KE-KE-SKI, Jesse, Whittier, NC, 70[?]; 6209, Celie, W, 63
26247 TEETESKII, Aggie, Robbinsville, NC, 24
16824 TESATESKA, Ella, Judson, NC, 21
16841 TESATEESKA, John, Robbinsville, NC, 56; Sampson, S, 15; Welch, S, 9; Lloyd, S, 7
16821 TESATESKA, Will, Robbinsville, NC, 49; 8424, Nancy, W, 45; Noah, S, 20; Mandy, D, 12
16297 TESATESKY, Noah, Robbinsville, NC, 30; 16297½, Eve, W, 18
9838 THOMAS, Alfred, Rome, GA, 72; Joseph H, S, 19; Ella Jane D, 28 [insane]
14568 THOMAS, Allie A, Round Mountain, AL, 20
15137 THOMAS, James A, Round Mountain, AL,46; Allen R, S, 18; Bearl L, D, 15; Hiram L, S, 11; Sallie, D, 6; Jack S, S, 5
10522 THOMAS, James H, Rome, GA, 35; William H, S, 18; Herbert H, S, 11; Annie J, D, 9; Stella, D, 5; Thomas Al S, 3; Harlin E, S, 1
11000 THOMAS, Mandy, Ducktown, TN, 33
36830 THOMASON, WB, Atlanta, GA, 21, 242 Sunset Ave; Lessie I, D, 1
42821 THOMPSON, Arsene, Swaine Co, NC, 22
16789 THOMPSON, Enis, Cherokee, NC, 43; 16249, Mandy, W, 44
24278 THOMPSON, Ernest, Charleston, WV, 39; Allison Garnett, S, 14; Ernest Trice, S, 12; Hugh Chas, S, 10
1262 THOMPSON, Martha, Culverson, NC, 32; Howard, S, 12; Mattie, D, 10; E, S, 7; Nebraskey, S, 5; Minnie, D, 8; Atha, D, 4; Jewell, S, 1; Marion, S, 1
1258 THOMPSON, Mary, Culberson, NC, 29; Iowa, S, 12; Olen, S, 9; Greely, S, 4; Vritis, S, 4; Iris, D, 1
39273 THRASHER, Ella V, Madola, GA, 66; Ethel, D, 1; Etta, D, 15; Lee, S, 13; Myrtle, D, 11; Thomas, S, 7; Paul, S, 5; Claud, S, 3; Flora, D, ½

EASTERN CHEROKEES RESIDING EAST OF MISSISSIPPI RIVER.

KEY: Guion Miller Application Number; Name; Address; Relation (to Head); Age in 1906

15856 TI-GOO-GI-DER, Ka-lu-qua-ta-ke, Cherokee, NC, 95 [Died 1907]
27357 TILLEY, Oma, Etowah, TN, 19
5058 TIMPSON, James, Murphy, NC, 51; Columbus H, S, 17; Callie May, S(?), 14
27308 TIMPSON, James A, Murphy, NC, 26
27309 TIMPSON, John S, Murphy, NC, 21
5057 TIMPSON, Umphrey P, Murphy, NC, 50

[TOHISKIE, Going Bird See #12755] *(Note: entry separate from other family groups)*

17597 TOINEETA, George, Cherokee, NC, 23
6214 TOINEETA, Loney, Cherokee, NC,46; 6638, Sally,W, 46; Martha,D,18; Caroline, D,13
6213 TOINEETA, Nick, Cherokee, NC, 39; 11120, Quatie, W, 44; Su-weg-ie, D, 18; Arneach, D, 14
28923 TOINEETA, West, Cherokee, NC, 25
15913 TOOMIE, Joseph, Wahhiyah, NC, 53; 16023, Engeline, W, 51; Andy, S, 14; Sa-la-lee-si, Susannah, And D, 5
27656 TOOMIE, Nick, Big Cove, NC, 25; 27631, Nancy, W, 28; Mary, D, 9; Nannie, D, Isaac, S, 2
31886 TOONIGH, Jukius(?), Wahhiyah, NC, 28
25980 TOONIGH, Mike, Cherokee, NC, 32; 11123, Anna, W, 28; Lige, S, 7; Nancy, D, 4
31885 TOONIGH, Nicey, Wahhiuah, NC, 33
11112 TOONIGH, Squency, Cherokee, NC, 54; 11159, Nancy, W, 44
13849 TREECE, Jessie A, Meltonsville, AL, 38, RFD #1; Henry R, S, 18; William D, S, 14; Mary E, D, 10; Daniel R, S, 8; Ethel M, D, 6
22957 TREW, Nora E, Euchee, TN, 25, RFD #1; Calsina, D, 6; Bigie R, S, 3
615 TROTT, John R, Verden, IL, 66
22432 TROTT, Wm O, Madison, IL, 39
11841 TROTTINGWOLF, Annie, Swayney, NC, 48
5950 TROTTINGWOLF, Katie, Cherokee, NC, 20
11839 TROTTINGWOLF, Moses, Swayney, NC,60
615 TROTT, John R, W, 48
22432 TROTT, Wm R, Swayney, NC, D, 17; Johnnie, S, 13

[TROTTINGWOLFE, Ned See #6033] *(Note: entry separate from other family groups)*

423 TUCKER, John M, Cherrylog, GA, 60
428 TUCKER, John W, Blue Ridge, GA, 36; James H, S, 10; John W, S, 8; Mary E, D, 5; Dewey S, S, 2
427 TUCKER, Mary P, Cherrylog, GA, 32; James L, S, 7
424 TUCKER, William P, Cherrylog, GA, 26
41630 TURNER, Emma Bell, Cartersville, GA, 19
749 TURNER, Lidora A, Cherrylog, GA, 39; James L, S, 11; John W, S, 9; Clifford, F, S, 6; Bertha P, D, 4

EASTERN CHEROKEES RESIDING EAST OF MISSISSIPPI RIVER.

KEY: Guion Miller Application Number; Name; Address; Relation (to Head); Age in 1906

15787 UTE, Andy, Whittier, NC, 53; 15777, Mary W, 58

44646 VAN, Katie, Lincoln, VA, 33
15748 VEAL, Sarah L, Quarles, Ga, 29; Harley, S, 11; Pratt, S, 9; Joseph, S, 7; Charley, S, 4; John, S, 2; William, S, 1
   41 VICK, Dora, Quarles, GA, 22; Andy M, S, 3; Lester, S, 1
   39 VICK, Mary, Quarles, GA, 26; Bessie, D, 8; Dessie, D, 5; Sallie, D, 3; Lockie, D, 2
20390 VOILES, Cora, Rossville, GA, 21
 3760 VOILES, Jane, Rossville, GA, 52; Jessie, D, 11; Jennie, D, 19; Bridy, D, 15
20632 VOILES, Vincent, Rossville, GA, 25; Annie M, D, 3
20389 VOILES, William, Rossville, GA, 23

[WADASUTTA, Anna See #11131]   *(Note: entry separate from other family groups)*

15828 WADDIE, Un-nigh, Swayney, NC, 62; 15830, Sol-ee-ol-ee-see, Waddie, W, 70
 6204 WADE, Bird, Judson, NC, 34; Lee, S, 3; Stewart, S, 1
15692 WADE, Davis, Whittier, NC, 39; 15687, Nancy, W, 30; Bird, S, 5
33066 WADE, Harold Clay, Allatoona, GA, 8; By Jos A Wade, Gdn
16828 WAGA, Annie, Cherokee, NC, 77
26246 WAH-CHECH-A, Jarrett or Grasshopper, Jarrett, Robbinsville, NC, 23
 3948 WAH-CHECH-A, Quelick, Robbinsville, NC, 49; 3949, Roxie, W, 30; Sarah, D, 18; Charley, S, 16; Jack, S, 14; Nancy, D, 14; Posey, D, 12; Susie, D, 10; John W, S, 8; Winnie, D, 6; Jess, S, 4; Onee, D, 2
26052 WAHHANEETA, Allen, Whittier, NC, 33; 16835, Sallie, W, 35; 26052, Posie, D, 4
 6190 WAHHANETA, John, Whittier, NC, 65; 7734, Caroline, W, 55
26053 WAHHANEETA, Samson, Whittier, NC, 23
34087 WAHHANEETA, William, Roddey, SC, 36; Maggie, D, 6; Samuel, S, 3

[WA-HOO, Elsie See #12748]   *(Note: entry separate from other family groups)*

10059 WAIHOO, Ned, Cherokee, NC, 38; Hattie, D, 9; Caroline, D 7; William, S, 5; Lizzie, D, 3
27580 WAKEFIELD, Albert Z, Andrews, NC, 27
24253 WAKEFIELD, Charley, Andrews, NC, 32
27579 WAKEFIELD, Edmon S, Andrews, NC, 29
24030 WAKEFIELD, Esco B, Andrews, NC, 39; Lucy May, D, 12; Lydia EM, D, 6; Albert McL, S, 2; Thos Alvin, S, 1
23695 WAKEFIELD, Kisy, Andrews, NC, 25
  916 WAKEFIELD, Lydia E, Andrews, NC, 65
23693 WAKEFIELD, Thomas M, Andrews, NC, 31
23694 WAKEFIELD, Virginia, Andrews, NC, 25
 2729 WALKER, Eudalia J, Dahlonega, GA, 30; Mamie, D, 8; John, S, 4; William, S, 3
16836 WALKINGSTICK, James, Birdtown, NC, 72; 16838, Matilda, W, 44
24575 WALKINGSTICK, James, Japan, NC, 23

EASTERN CHEROKEES RESIDING EAST OF MISSISSIPPI RIVER.

KEY: Guion Miller Application Number; Name; Address; Relation (to Head); Age in 1906

24574 WALKINGSTICK, Jasper, Japan, NC, 34; 12794, Annie, W, 25; Nation, S, 3; Maggie, D, 1
15842 WALKINGSTICK, John, Birdtown, NC, 48; 15839, Walsie, W, 34; Owen, S, 17; Maggie, D, 15; Mose, S, 10; Celie, D, 8; Mike, S, 4; Thomas, S, 2
6219 WALKINGSTICK, Mike, Japan, NC, 69; 16819, Caroline, W, 54; Bascum, S, 17
39477 WALLACE, Olly, Cherokee, NC, 41
3946 WARD, Charles J, Ellijay, GA, 39; Jennie May, D, 16
979 WARD, Clara A, New York City, NY, 47, 29 W 38th St
5482 WARLICK, Mary Jane, Murphy, NC, 38; Edna May, D, 7
16330 WASHINGTON, Jesse, Cherokee, NC, 31; 16796, Ollie Ann, W, 33; Reed, Lizzie, D of W, 13; 16330, Washington, Luzane, D, 7; Rachel, D, 4; Emma, D, 1
16809 WASHINGTON, Joseph, Cherokee, NC, 32, By Lizzie Washington, Mother
15853 WASHINGTON, Key, Cherokee, NC, 48
16791 WASHINGTON, Lizzie, Cherokee, NC, 58
3005 WATERS, Polly, Cleveland, TN, 71
15826 WATTY, John, Swayney, NC, 15, By Ute Watty, Gdn
29763 WATY, Lidge, Swayney, NC, 29; 29764, Nancy, W, 31; Steve, S, 8; Royeenih, D, 7; Lizzie, D, 5; Wallie, D, 1
27226 WATY, Nute, Swayney, NC, 43; 7754, Mary, W, 37
10062 WAYNE, William J, Cherokee, NC, 34
26948 WEBB, Annie E, Knoxville, TN, 22
1468 WEBB, Emily Cherokee, Knoxville, TN, 58
26949 WEBB, James C, Knoxville, TN, 25
26951 WEBB, John H, Knoxville, TN, 28
26947 WEBB, Letcher P, Benton, TN, 33
26950 WEBB, Robert A, Knoxville, TN, 30
1259 WEBSTER, Rachel A, Culberson, NC, 65
1261 WEBSTER, William L, Culberson, NC, 36; Jetter, S, 9; Carrie, D, 6; 1261, Webster, Norma, Culberson, NC, S(?), 4; William R, S, 1
12174 WEINMAN, Jennie EL, Macon, GA, 9, 319 Hazel St, By Geo B, Weinman, Gdn
15816 WELCH, Adam, Wahhiyah, NC, 20; 16029, Anna E, W, 14
11117 WELCH, Charlotte, Cherokee, NC, 19; William H, Bro, 17; James, Bro, 15; Lucinda, Sis, 13;   By John Goins Welch, Gdn
16888 WELCH, Corneta, Carlisle, PA, 26
15847 WELCH, Davis W, Wahhiyah, NC, 38; 36186, Eve, W, 37; John, S, 18; James, S, 16; Jesse, S, 14; Joseph, S, 7; Ned, S, 3; Lizzie, D, 1
28471 WELCH, Eddie, Birdtown, NC, 21; 15714, Sarah J, W, 19
28370 WELCH, Epps, Birdtown, NC, 22; 15795, Stacy, W, 16
5445 WELCH, Jackson, Tomotla, NC, 36; 27581, Sallie, W, 26; Eddie R, S, 4; Nannie, D, 1
17701 WELCH, John, Tomotla, NC, 14; Mary, Sis, 16;   By Jackson Welch, Gdn
6636 WELCH, John G, Cherokee, NC, 62
13161 WELCH, Madeline G, Camden, NJ, 25[?], 411 Market St
24443 WELCH, Mary, Japan, NC, 41; Axe, Lucinda, D, 18; Peter, S, 12; Mandy, D, 10; Welch, Lee, S, 3

EASTERN CHEROKEES RESIDING EAST OF MISSISSIPPI RIVER.

KEY: Guion Miller Application Number; Name; Address; Relation (to Head); Age in 1906

- **7733** WELCH, Mary E, Cherokee, NC, 33; Lloyd R, S, 12; Theodore A, S, 10; Clarence, S, 8; Robin, Richard, S, 3
- **6508** WELCH, Sampson, Birdtown, NC, 47; 10414, Arlicke, W, 46; Jane, D, 16; Nannie, D, 13
- **15706** WENN, John, Birdtown, NC, 51; 15702, Nancy, W, 49
- **15701** WESLEY, Judas, Birdtown, NC, 24; 15703, Jinnie, W, 50
- **31214** WEST, Faustina E, Andrews, NC, 32
- **6509** WEST, Michael, Birdtown, NC, 23
- **29973** WESTFIELD, Fannie, Grief, TN, 31; Mollie, D, 16; Ralph, S, 14; Elihu, S, 10; Reese, S, 4
- **17856** WHIPPERWILL, Allen, Cherokee, NC, 26
- **11136** WHIPPERWILL, Manly W, Cherokee, NC, 22
- **35450** WHISENANT, Emma, Keener, AL, 30; Presley, S, 12; Vester, S, 9; Dewey, S, 7; Creola, D, 5; Lola, D, 3; Vinnie, D, 1
- **361** WHITAKER, David L, Andrews, NC, 68
- **1481** WHITAKER, James M, Andrews, NC, 60
- **27791** WHITAKER, Martha A, Andrews, NC, 64 [Deceased By Mack Cooper, Adm]
- **2664** WHITAKER, Rutha, Andrews, NC, 27; Ada, D, 8; Jud, S, 6
- **1480** WHITAKER, Sarah A, Andrews, NC, 58
- **3922** WHITAKER, Stephen D, Andrews, NC, 51
- **27153** WHITE, Anda J, Kosh, AL, 22; Walter A, S, 3; Bessie E, D, 1
- **9830** WHITE, Bettie, Andrews, NC, 17; Dillard, S, 2; Dee, S, 1
- **23475** WHITFIELD, Emma C, Chattanooga, TN, 35, 6 MacMillion Ave; Johnson, Thomas C, S, 13; James N, S, 11; Richard C, S, 9; Anna R, D, 7
- **24799** WHITT, Callie, Cumming, GA, 21, RFD #1; Gurney, S, 2
- **29399** WIGGINS, Estelle R, Bryson City, NC, 22; Mildred, D, 1
- **15691** WILD CAT, Birdtown, NC, 61; 15695, Rebecca, W, 61

[WILDCAT, Testie See #29397]   *(Note: entry separate from other family groups)*

- **24464** WILDCAT, Tinola, Birdtown, NC, 25; 15837, Alsie, W, 40
- **4141** WILKINSON, Jefferson, Flintstone, GA, 23
- **4142** WILKINSON, William, High Point, GA, 32; Silvester, S, 3; Wayman, S, 1
- **15696** WILL, John, Birdtown, NC, 50; 15835, Jane, W, 37; 15696, Mooney, S, 12; James, S, 5; Alice, D, 3
- **23110** WILLIAMS, Claud, Hill City, TN, 26; Fred M, S, 1
- **273** WILLIAMS, Daniel M, Isabella, TN, 36; Jessie, D, 14; May, D, 7; Robert, S, 4
- **274** WILLIAMS, James DM, Isabella, TN, 27; Wm M, S, 6; Robert, S, 1
- **30337** WILLIAMS, James Fred, Atlanta, GA, 32, 195 Crew St
- **3508** WILLIAMS, John HF, Sweden, GA, 25; Charley, S, 6; Arvey, S, 4; Clifford, S, 2
- **6028** WILLIAMS, Mollie O, Flowery Branch, GA, 39
- **22769** WILLIS, Andrew E, Dawsonville, GA, 42; Mary, D, 3; Benny, S, 2; Early, S, 1/12
- **159** WILLIS, Pickens E, Dawsonville, GA, 76
- **15896** WILNOTY, Joe, Cherokee, NC, 12,   By Annie Littlejohn, Gdn
- **15815** WILNOTY, Mink, Big Cove, NC, 66

EASTERN CHEROKEES RESIDING EAST OF MISSISSIPPI RIVER.

KEY: Guion Miller Application Number; Name; Address; Relation (to Head); Age in 1906

16799 WILNOTY, Moses, Cherokee, NC, 20
15897 WILNOTY, Ned, Cherokee, NC, 10, By Annie Littlejohn, Gdn
16303 WILNOTY, Ned, Birdtown, NC, 53; 16334, Sallie, W, 57
16800 WILNOTY, Lanty, Cherokee, NC, 58; Nice, D, 18; Sammon, S, 14; Haggie, D, 2
31177 WILSON, Margaret N, Avondale, TN, 26, 215 Roane St; Roscoe, S, 5; Ancil, S, 3; Edna M, D, 1
1415 WILSON, Mary, Dayton, TN, 50
27345 WILSON, Rosalee, Heliotrope, TN, 34; Jefferson, S, 11; Luther, S, 10; Monnie, D, 8; Mary, D, 7; Minnie, D, 5; Selma, D, 3; Arthur, S, 2
1777 WISHON, George, Ballplay, TN, 45
1780 WISHON, John W, Cherrylog, GA, 53; Bertha G, D, 17; Gaily O, D, 13
1794 WISHON, Robert C, Cherrylog, GA, 29
1795 WISHON, Thomas J, Cherrylog, GA, 23
1778 WISHON, William T, Cherrylog, GA, 51; Willis D, S, 18; Pelmina M, D, 15; Charity M, D, 14; John W, Jr, S, 12; George W, S, 11; McKinley E, S, 8; Martha E, D, 7; Charley M, S, 6
15910 WOLFE, Amanda W, Rising Sun, MD, 16
15909 WOLFE, Charles Hicks, Wahhiyah, NC, 14, By Jasper Wolfe, Brother
6224 WOLFE, David, Birdtown, NC, 65[?]
16026 WOLFE, Elkiny, Wahhiyah, NC, 24
20617 WOLFE, Francis M, Harrison, TN, 44; John Albert, S, 16; Estella, D, 14
15906 WOLFE, George L, Birdtown, NC, 29; John R, S, 4; William H, S, 2; Richard C, S, 1
11842 WOLF, Jacob, Swayney, NC, 35; 11840, Nelcena, W, 33; Laura, D, 16; Rachel, D, 13; James, S, 10; Joseph, S, 9; Jesse, S, 7; Abel, S, 3

[WOLFE, James See Roll #2760]   *(Note: entry separate from other family groups)*
   (NOTE: Unable to locate application number)

20618 WOLFE, James L, Oltewah, TN, 36
15908 WOLFE, James T, Wahhiyah, NC, 19

[WOLFE, Jennie See Roll #2760]   *(Note: entry separate from other family groups)*
   (NOTE: Unable to locate application number)

[WOLFE, Martha See Roll #2761]   *(Note: entry separate from other family groups)*
   (NOTE: Unable to locate application number)

[WOLFE, Johnnie See #22432]   *(Note: entry separate from other family groups)*

11121 WOLFE, John, Wahhiyah, NC 39; 11127, Wolfe, Linda, W, 28; Walker, S, 1
15836 WOLFE, John, Birdtown, NC, 31; 23883 Callie, W, 33
7750 WOLFE, Johnson, Wahhiyah, NC, 37; 31496, Mattie, W; Job, S, 4; Edison, S, 2
10066 WOLFE, Joseph, Wahhiyah, NC, 35; 10080, Jennie, W, 36; Kelly, S, 8
11145 WOLFE, Jowen, Wahhiyah, NC, 47; 11143, Sallie, W, 48
11156 WOLFE, Kinsey, Swayney, NC, 21

EASTERN CHEROKEES RESIDING EAST OF MISSISSIPPI RIVER.

KEY: Guion Miller Application Number; Name; Address; Relation (to Head); Age in 1906

441 WOLFE, Louis Henry, Louisville, TN, 34; Delia Ann, D, 15; Louis David, S, 13; Sophronia Isabel, D, 10; Manda Jane, D, 7; Eliza Pauline, D, 4; James William, S, 1/6
15911 WOLFE, Margaret P, Carlisle, PA, 18
38691 WOLFE, Mary, Harrison, TN, 5; Mattie, sis, 3; By Annie Wolf, Gdn
15912 WOLFE, Mary E, Carlisle, PA, 24

[WOLFE, Mollie See #10055]   *(Note: entry separate from other family groups)*

[WOLFE, Moses See #11839]   *(Note: entry separate from other family groups)*

[WOLFE, Lloyd See #10055]   *(Note: entry separate from other family groups)*

[WOLFE, Emmaneatte See #10055]
[WOLFE, Thomas See #10055]   *(Note: entry separate from other family groups)*
[WOLFE, Jinsey See #10055]

7742 WOLF, Owen, Wahhiyah, NC, 25[?]
10077 WOLFE, Polly, Wahhiyah, NC, 61
16024 WOLFE, Sallie, Wahhiyah, NC, 81
12774 WOLFE, Susan, Wahhiyah, NC, 55; Ward, S, 14
42563 WOOD, Hester O, Collinsville, IL, 13
31261 WOOD, Rachel, Boaz, AL, 52
1523 WRIGHT, George W, Galloway, GA, 62; James, S, 18
32188 WRIGHT, Mando, Jellico, TN, 31; Nellie, D, 3; Yone, S, 1
32714 WRIGHT, Sally, Galloway, GA, 29
32715 WRIGHT, Thomas, Galloway, GA, 21
28183 WYLY, Robert M, Chattanooga, TN, 23; 517 Leonard St

11138 YANAGUSKI, Lizzie, Wahhiyah, NC, 36
12750 YOUNCE, Nancy S, Birdtown, NC, 54; Nancy E, D, 17; Dasie M, D, 15
16251 YOUNGBIRD, John, Cherokee, NC, 46; 16324, Dinah, W, 48; 16251, Rufus, S, 19; Soggy, S, 16; Yah-nih, S, 14; Wesley, S, 12; James, S, 5; Wal-gin-nih, S, 1
36986 YOUNGDEER, Jesse, Cherokee, NC, 22
16250 YOUNGDEER, John, Cherokee, NC, 53; 16833, Betsy, W, 50; Steve, S, 15; Onnie, D, 13; Mattie, D, 11; Moody, S, 10

THE EASTERN CHEROKEES vs THE UNITED STATES

No. 23,214

Supplemental Roll of Eastern Cherokees

JANUARY 5, 1910

List of names to be added to and stricken from the original roll Eastern Cherokees as reported on May 28, 1909, as recommended by Guion Miller, Special Commissioner, in his supplemental report of January 5, 1910, together with certain clerical corrections to be made in the original roll.

SUPPLEMENTAL ROLL of
EASTERN CHEROKEES RESIDING EAST OF MISSISSIPPI RIVER.

KEY: Guion Miller Application Number, Name, Address, Relation (to Head), Age in 1906.

ABERNATHY, Minnie, Cartersville, GA, 34; Matterson, S, 13; Carry, D, 10; Mandy, D, 7; Jefry[sic], S, 4; Roosevelt, S, 2; Ollie, D, 1
ADAMS, Carrie F, Washington, DC, 35 3156 18th St. NW; Leo D, S, 17; Willie H, S, 16; James H, S, 13; Fred M, S, 9; Ruth B, D, 5

[ADAMS, Lula. See #32042]

39636   ARENDALE, Lovie, Hedwig, GA, 33; Belle, D, 12; Kate, D, 7; Erolene, D, 5; Russell, S, 3; Leona, D, 1

43768   BEAVER, Inas, Unaka, NC, 14; Leander, Bro, 9; Lillie, Sis, 4; Gay, Sis 1; Greely, Bro, 1   By Alice Beaver, mother
15356   BECK, Cooper, Canton, GA, 20
41888   BECK, G. Perinole, Spartansburg, SC, 34; Jenett, D, 6; Lucile, D, 3; Nora, D, 1
15355   BECK, Jeff, Canton, GA, 27; Willie H, 4
15354   BECK, Johnie, Canton, GA, 15
11341   BECK, Martin V, Burtsboro, GA, 57; Lila May, D, 4; Laura, D, 3
15353   BECK, Namon, Canton, GA, 21
         BENNETT, Jessie, Plainsville, GA, 13; Addie L, Sis, 10; Lillie May, Sis, 5; Gracie, Sis, 1   By Alice Bennett, Gdn. And mother
         BLACKFOX, Cah-lah-tah-yih, Cherokee, NC, 24
         BLYTHE, Sampson, Cherokee, NC, 3   By Arch Blythe, parent and Gdn.

[BOONE, Betsie H. See 2803]

35946   BRADLEY, Johnson, Cherokee, NC, 26
13188   BRADY. Robert A, Topton, NC, 38; Eliza, D, 11; Sarah, D, 10; Arthur, S, 8; McKinley, S, 5; Luther, S, 3; Elizabeth, D, 1
         BRAY, Nellie, Sequatchie, TN, 9; Jesse, Bro, 7 By Margaret M. Chadwick, Gdn.
         BURDETTE, Barilla P. Atlanta, GA, 21, R.F.D. #5
32622   BURGESS, Olie, Grapecreek, NC, 25; James, S, 8; Van, S, 6; Martha, D, 4; Mary, D, 4; Arthur, S, 1; John, S, 2
15214   BURNS, Henewee, Canton, GA, 28; 15215 Jack, S, 2; 15218 Marie, D, 6
         BYRD, Leona, Rome, GA, 17 [Dau. Of #2631]

34582   CAMPBELL, Lurita, Murphy, NC, 17
28268   CHADWICK, Margaret M, Sequatchie, TN, 54; Delia, D, 18; Ruby, D, 16
         CHADWICK, William E, Sequatchie, TN, 33
45230   COMPTON, Juliette C.H. Columbus, GA, 41, 212 16th St.
         COOPER, Raymond F, St. Elmo, TN, 16; Allie D, Sis, 13; William G, Bro, 11   By Laura A. Cooper, parent and Gdn.

SUPPLEMENTAL ROLL of
EASTERN CHEROKEES RESIDING EAST OF MISSISSIPPI RIVER.

KEY: Guion Miller Application Number, Name, Address, Relation (to Head), Age in 1906.

CRAIG, William, Cherokee, NC, 21

30761 DARLAN, Harriet, Grapecreek, NC, 35; McDonald, Robert, S, 16; Mack, S, 14; Darlan, Bessie, D, 12; Will Mc, S, 6
43 DAVIS, Arvaline, Blue Ridge, GA, 16; Marion, D, 1
DUNLAP, Mary A, Bryson City, NC, 52

GILL, Noah, Rockwood, TN, 17; Ludie, Bro, 15; Robbie, Bro, 13; Charlie, Bro, 5 By Calsina Gill, parent and Gdn.
GILL, Shelly, Rockwood, TN, 23

15265 HAGGARD, Sandle T, Sparta, TN, 30; Mary F, D, 11; Myrtle G, D, 4; Nellie M, D, 2
14965 HARRIS, John A, Huntsville, AL, 50, 416 Stephens Ave.; John E, S, 9; George W, S, 5; Mary L, D, 1
34582 HARTNESS, Julia, Murphy, NC, 21
15261 HAYGOOD, Carrie, Canton, GA, 26
HORNBUCKLE, Artie, Cherokee, NC, 16
45382 HUDSON, Ellen S.L, Columbus, GA, 31, 1531 3rd Ave.
45383 HUDSON, Thomas Charlton, Columbus, GA, 28 1531 3rd Ave.

34582 JAMES, Asa, Murphy, NC, 19; Allen, Bro, 9
JESSON, John, Newtown, PA, 30
JOHNSON, Isaac, Wahhiyah, NC, 13
JOHNSON, Tempa, Cherokee, NC, 16

KILLGORE, Eulalie, Victoria, TN, 28; Eula, D, 10; Lena, D, 7
26220 KIRKSEY, Eugene, Sulphur Springs, AL, 33
11631 KIRKSEY, Fanny, Sulphur Springs, AL, 74
26218 KIRKSEY, Florence M, Sulphur Springs, AL, 39
26217 KIRKSEY, Isabella, Sulphur Springs, AL, 50
29216 KIRKSEY, Mary, Sulphur Springs, AL, 52
26219 KIRKSEY, Mattie, Sulphur Springs, AL, 35
26215 KIRKSEY, William W, Sulphur Springs, AL, 47; Reuben L, S, 8; Jewell M, D, 6; George B.M, S, 4; Alvin M, S, 1

26407 LANGLEY, Frank C, Plainsville, GA, 23; Minnie Lee, S, 3
LEDFORD, Polly, Almond, NC, 25
12795 LITTLE JOHN, Sally Anne, Cherokee, NC, 4; Sow-wah-nee, Bro, 2; Toonie, Legilly, N of W, 12; Little John, Goo-lah-gee, Bro, 7
By Elowih Little John, parent and Gdn.
LONG, Rachel, Cherokee, NC, 24

SUPPLEMENTAL ROLL of
EASTERN CHEROKEES RESIDING EAST OF MISSISSIPPI RIVER.

KEY: Guion Miller Application Number, Name, Address, Relation (to Head), Age in 1906.

2766   LOW, Mary Rogers, Duluth, GA, 20 By John J. Low, father and Gdn.

30964   McDONALD, Andy, Brady, NC, 23; Robert, S, 1
29731   McDONALD, James, Grapecreek, NC, 27
30809   McDONALD, John, Jr, Grapecreek, NC, 33; May, D, 7; Addie, D, 5

[McDONALD, Robert. See Roll #30330]
    (Unable to locate Application number)

[McDONALD, Mack. See #30331
    (Unable to locate Application number)

30710   McDONALD, West, Ogreeta, NC, 31; Walter, S, 10; Myrtle, D, 8; Loyd, S, 6; Hobert, S, 2

        MANEY, Eve Wilnoty, Cherokee, NC, 20; Mary, D, 2; John, S, 1
        MARTIN, Hubert M, Chattanooga, TN, 7 6 and Cross Sts.
        By James G. Martin, parent and Gdn.
        MARTIN, Paul H, Chattanooga, TN, 7; Edith M, Sis, 5
        By William W. Martin, parent and Gdn.
30763   MASHBURN, Susan, Vests, NC, 27; Bertha, D, 10; Kate, D, 8; Florence, D, 6; Norma, D, 2
        MEE, Katie Van.
25548   MILLER, Flonnie A, Marble, NC, 17
34645   MORGAN, Orange, Loudon, TN, 55
        MORRISON, Della, Victoria, TN, 23; Fred, S, 6; Myrtle, D, 4; Patty Edgar, S, 3; Eddie, S, 1
        MUMBLEHEAD, Tawney, Almond, NC, 24
6646   MURPHY, David, Johnson City, TN, 88 Soldiers' Home.
21096   MURPHY, Isabella, Nina, NC, 27
11399   MURPHY, Jane, Unaka, NC, 30; Walter, S, 9
6015   MURPHY, Leander, Unaka, NC: 52; 44802 Joe, S, 13; Mandie, D, 5 [Died 9-1907]
28652   MURPHY, Louisa, Apalachia, NC, 20
24397   MURPHY, Manco, Unaka, NC, 41
6014   MURPHY, Martin, Unaka, NC, 73
6013   MURPHY, Sollie, Apalachia, NC, 50; Margaret, D, 19; Maneve, S, 17; Howard, S, 14; Willard, S, 1

        OOKUMMA, Annie, Cherokee, NC, 19
        OTTER, Allen, Almond, NC: 35

[OWEN, Isabell McD. See #6960]

SUPPLEMENTAL ROLL of
EASTERN CHEROKEES RESIDING EAST OF MISSISSIPPI RIVER.

KEY: Guion Miller Application Number, Name, Address, Relation (to Head), Age in 1906.

   OWL, Mandy, Cherokee, NC, 24
10067 OWL, Tahquette, Cherokee, NC, 3 By Ollie Jackson, parent and Gdn.

43853 PARKER, Colquit, Summerville, GA, 24
38186 PARKER, Roxey, Toney, AL, 20
   PARKER, Taylor, Rome, GA, 18 Care Sharp & Sharp
   PARKER, William, Rome, GA, 24
43898 PATTERSON, Iowa, Shooting Creek, NC, 23; Josie, D, 6; Lura, D, 3
32470 PHILYAW, Jennie, Tate, Ga, 29; Dewey, S, 8; Enner, S, 2
15316 PUCKETT, Ella, Canton, GA, 23; Lula May, D, 5; Roy, S, 3; George, S, 1

   ROGERS, Mamie E, Wolf Creek, NC, 5
   By Cordelia Rogers, parent and Gdn.

   SAUNOOKE, Annie, Cherokee, NC, 26
6379 SMITH, Alice, Tellico Plains, TN, 25; Lester, S, 6; May, D, 3
   SMITH, Arthur, Walland, TN, 23
   SMITH, Garfield, Walland, TN, 21
7744 SMITH, Louraine, Birdtown, NC, 44
34189 SMITH, Mary Melvinie, Cherokee, NC, 53
8423 SMITH, Sam, Birdtown, NC, 43; Susie, D, 19; Blaine, S, 17; Joe, S, 15
   Belva, D, 13; Goldman, S, 10; Dave, S, 8; Jesse, S, 6
34790 STILES, Mary J, Apalachia, NC, 21; Omiu, S, 5; Thomas, S, 3; Nina, D, 1
   SWIMMER, John, Cherokee, NC, 23
   SWIMMER, Mary, Cherokee, NC, 46

15138 THOMAS, Donor, Anniston, AL, 23, 1929 Gurnee St.; Snow Belle, D, 2
   Pauline, D, 1
   THOMPSON, Lydia, Cherokee, NC, 17; Wilson, Bro, 15; Goliath, Bro, 10
   By Enis Thompson, parent and Gdn.
   THOMPSON, Peter, Cherokee, NC, 18

[TOONIE, Legilly. See #12795]

   TRAMPER, Ammons, Cherokee, NC, 20
   TRAMPER, Chiltoski, Carlisle, PA, 25 Care Indian School
   TRAMPER, Lottie, Carlisle, PA, 14 Care Indian School

3948 WAH-CHECH-A, Jim or Grasshopper, Robbinsville, NC, 20
   [Son of #2815
   WAIHOO, Sally A, Cherokee, NC, 31

[WAYNE, Sarah [John]. See #10039]

SUPPLEMENTAL ROLL of
EASTERN CHEROKEES RESIDING EAST OF MISSISSIPPI RIVER.

KEY: Guion Miller Application Number, Name, Address, Relation (to Head), Age in 1906.

26949   WEBB, Eleanor L, Knoxville, TN, 2. 993 Gratz St.
         By James C. Webb, parent and Gdn.
26947   WEBB, Ethel, Knoxville, TN, 7; Florence A, Sis, 6
         By Letcher P. Webb, father and Gdn.
         WELCH, Mark G, Conway, MA, 29

[WILLIAMS, Jennie. See #1103]

         YONCE, Georgia, Birdtown, NC, 3   By Katherine Lambert, Gdn.
16569   YOUNG, Mollie, Springplace, GA, 33; Kirby, S, 9; John J, S, 3; Dora M, D, 1
         YOUNGDEER, Jacob, Cherokee, NC, 26
16250   YOUNGDEER, Jonah, Cherokee, NC, 28; Eli, Bro, 25 [Incompetent]
         By John Youngdeer, parent and Gdn.

THE FOLLOWING NAMES, ORIGINALLY ENROLLED AS ENTITLED TO PARTICIPATE IN THE FUND, ORDERED BY THE COURT OF CLAIMS TO BE STRICKEN FROM THE ROLL OF MAY 28, 1909.

KEY: Guion Miller Application Number; Name; Address; Relation (to Head); Age in 1906

31260   GOBLE, James, Albertville, AL, 21 [Duplicate]

15704   SMITH, Jessie, Cherokee, NC, 14; Mandy, ?, 11; Martha, ?, 10

3721   ADAIR, May E, Stilwell, OK, 17; George W, Bro, 15; Samuel W, Bro, 13; Lula E, Sis, 11; Lilly E, Sis, 8   [Duplicates]

41210   CHANDLER, William P, Tahlequah, OK, 35

28252   JORDAN, Felix R, Collinsville, OK, 17   [Duplicate]

36166   JORDAN, Mollie, Collinsville, OK, 15   [Duplicate]

37062   KRIGBAUM, James A, Coweta, OK, 7   [Duplicate]

12530   LOWERY, Susie, Muskogee, OK, 17; Elsie J, Sis, 14; Andrew, Bro, 12; Henry C, Bro, 7   [Duplicates]

12892   LYNCH, Nancy E, Bunch, OK, 1   [Duplicate]

13701   MABRY, Sallie B, Briertown, OK, 47

40048   RYAN, Emmett, Proctor, OK, 10; Calvin, ?, 8; William, ?, 5   [Duplicates]

34463   SCALES, Mattie, Flint, OK, 38; Grover, S, 17; Joseph, S, 15; Lillie, D, 12; Louisa, D, 10; George, S, 7; Ann L, D, 3; Mary E, D, 5/12

18862   SMITH, Lee, Braggs, OK, 17; Arch, Bro, 14; Mattie, Sis, 11   [Duplicates]

31995   STEWART, Celina K, Grove, OK, 60

31998   STEWART, George W, Bluejacket, OK, 24

31996   STEWART, John H, Bluejacket, OK, 34; Max, S, 6

31997   STEWART, William W, Grove, OK, 31

8233   SWEANEY, John T, Eugene, MO, 32

175   SWIMMER, Louisa, Rose, OK, 17   [Duplicate]

THE FOLLOWING NAMES, ORIGINALLY ENROLLED AS ENTITLED TO PARTICIPATE IN THE FUND, ORDERED BY THE COURT OF CLAIMS TO BE STRICKEN FROM THE ROLL OF MAY 28, 1909.

KEY: Guion Miller Application Number; Name; Address; Relation (to Head); Age in 1906

13564   VICTORY, Samuel, Collinsville, OK, 19; Charles, Bro, 17; Susan, Sis, 15; Andrew, Bro, 13; Anna A, Sis, 10; Donney, Sis, 9; Tensy, Sis, 20 [Duplicates]

3005   WATERS, Polly, Cleveland TN, 71

5011   WILLIAMS, Louisa, Tyro, KS, 55   [Duplicate]

Index

ABERNATHY
  Carry 41
  Jefry 41
  Mandy 41
  Matterson 41
  Minnie 41
  Ollie 41
  Roosevelt 41
ADAIR
  George W 46
  Lilly E 46
  Lula E 46
  May E 46
  Samuel W 46
ADAMS
  Adaline 1
  Carrie F 41
  Ethel E 1
  Frank 1
  Fred M 41
  Gudger 1
  Harry 1
  Ina 1
  James H 41
  John V 1
  Leo D 41
  Lewie 1
  Lula 41
  Monell 1
  Nora 1
  Rolling 1
  Ruth B 41
  Vinia 1
  Walter 1
  Willard 1
  Willie H 41
AH-HIH-DAH 1
ALEXANDER
  Geo M 1
  George M 16
  Jeannie M 1
  Jennie M 16
ALLEN
  Emmerline 1

  Eve 1
  John 1
  Junn-lus-kie 1
  Rebecca 1
  Sallie 1
  Will 1
ALLISON
  Albert Monroe 1
  Nannie 1
  Roy Robert 1
ALTON
  Burduir 1
  Claude 1
  James 1
  John 1
  Kate 1
  Liney 1
  McKinley 1
  Texas 1
ANDERSON
  Bertha 1
  Bessie R 1
  Beulah 1
  Cora Neal 1
  Cora O 1
  Eddie W 1
  Eulah 1
  Jane 1
  Lillie May 1
  Rannie 1
  Wilber E 1
ARCH
  David 1
  Jennie 1
  Johnson 1
  Martha 1
  Ollivan 1
  Ross 1
ARENDALE
  Belle 41
  Erolene 41
  Kate 41
  Leona 41
  Lovie 41

49

Index

Russell 41
ARMACHAIN
   Anna 1
   Anna Eliza 1
   Annie 1
   Conseen 1
   Davis 1
   Jesse 1
   Jonie 1
   Kahida 1
   Lacy 1
   Lewel 1
   Ollie 1
   Rachel 1
   Severe 1
   Susie 1
ARNEACH
   Anna 1
   Bessie 1
   Buck 1
   James K 1
   Jefferson 1
   Jenny 1
   Lizzie 1
   Mary 1
   Nell 1
   Sarah 1
   Will W 1
ARNOLD
   Allie 1
   Arthur 1
   Beckie 1
   Do 1
   Dock 1
   Henry 1
   Jess 1
   John 1
   Lula 1
   Martha 1
   Prince 1
   Ruby 1
ASAY
   Sarah Diannah 1
ASHMAN

   Laura 1
ATKINS
   Bennie Weaver 2
   Emmet D 1
   James M 1
   James Wm 1
   Lillian J 2
   Mary F 2
   Ruth D 2
AUSTIN
   Alice 2
   Jackson 2
   James 2
   Lelah 2
   Maggie 2
   Nana 2
AXE
   Amos 2
   Caroline 2
   David 2
   Eighty 2
   Eva 2
   Jennie 2
   John D 2
   Josiah 2
   Lucinda 2, 37
   Maggie 2
   Mandy 2, 37
   Nancy 2
   Peter 2, 37
   Sam Smoker 2
   Sarah 2
   Willie 2

BAGWELL
   Carl 2
   Carrie 2
   Florence 2
   Francis E 2
   Hoydt 2
   John Berry 2
   Joseph A 2
   Kate 2
   Pearl 2

Index

Susie 2
BAKER
  Arthur 2
  Charley 2
  Cricket 2
  Dona 2
  Elizabeth 2
  Ellen M 2
  Elmira 2
  Luther 2
  Mary 2
  Mary A 2
  Stella 2
  Worldly 2
BARKSDALE
  Belle 2
  Jewry 2
  Mabel 2
BARNS
  Barney 2
  Galley 2
  Mary 2
BARNWELL
  Carleton 2
  Elizabeth 2
  Middleton S 2
  Stephen E 2
BARRETT
  Clara J 2
  Mary Alice 2
BATTLE
  Adaline E 2
  Addie E 2
  Bruce W 2
  Laura E 2
  Lox V 2
  William M 2
  Zed P 2
BAUER
  Fred B 2
  Owenah A 2
BEAN
  Ollie 2
BEARMEAT
  Mary 2
BEAVER
  Alice 41
  Gay 41
  Greely 41
  Inas 41
  Leander 41
  Lillie 41
BECK
  Berry B 2
  Cooper 41
  Edith D 2
  Emory S 2
  Eugene W 3
  Fletcher 2
  G Perinole 41
  James 2
  Jeff 41
  Jenett 41
  Johnie 41
  Laura 41
  Lila May 41
  Lillie F 2
  Lucile 41
  Major J 3
  Martin V 41
  Mary A 2
  May D 3
  Namon 41
  Nancy S 2
  Noah 2
  Nora 41
  Rose 3
  Samuel 3
  Samuel, Jr 3
  Sarah 3
  Savannah G 3
  Thomas 3
  Willie H 41
BEDDIX
  Mary Jane 3
  Rose 3
BELL
  Ada Jane 3

Index

Albert M 3
Anice 3
Basil R 3
Edward E 3
Eleanor B 3
George A 3
Harley E 3
Henry Charlton 3
Isla May 3
John 3
Lucile 3
Mary Jane 3
Mary McDair 3
Raymond B 3
Reuben E 3
Rubey 3
Virgil E 3
Walter L 3
Wilber P 3
Willard 3
William A 3
BEN
Cheech 3
Ollie 3
Stand 3
BENGE
Hooley 3
May 3
Mitchell 3
Richard 3
Samson 3
BENNETT
Addie L 41
Alice 3
Allice 41
Gracie 41
Jessie 41
Lillie May 41
BENSON
Alonzo M 3
Ezekiel 3
Horner H 3
Leslie 3
Moye 3
Rebecca M 3
BETTIS
Harriet Anna 3
James H 3
Nellie Jim 3
Ralph K 3
Robert Knox 3
Roy Henry 3
Virgil 3
BIGMEAT
Adam 3
Auneka 3
Isaiah 3
Minda 3
Nancy 3
Nickademas 3
Robert 3
Sarah 3
Yona 3
BIGWITCH
Alice 3
Charlie 3
Joseph 3
Lucy 3
Sallie Long 3
BIRD
Annie 4
Bessie 4
Bettie 4
Bird C 3
Colinda 3
Dan 3, 4
David 1, 4
Eli 4
Going 4
Lize 4
Lizzie 4
Loyd 4
Nan 3
Ollie 3
Olliw 4
Polly 4
Quattie 4
Sill 4

Index

Solomon 4
Spencer 4
Steve 4
Timpson 4
Tohiskie 4
Wallie 4
BLACK
Arthur C 4
John H 4
Mary E 4
Roy R 4
William E 4
BLACKFOX
Cah-lah-tah-yih 41
Charles 4
Cindy 4
Diahnah 4
Joe 4
Josiah 4
Lloyd 4
BLANKENSHIP
Rebecca A 4
BLYTHE
Adelia 4
Arch 4, 41
David 4
Elizabeth 4
James 4
Jarrett 4
Josephine 2
Lillie J 4
Louisia C 4
Nannie 4
Riley C 4
Sampson 41
Stella 4
Will Johnson 4
William H 4
BOND
Elisha 4
Emogene 4
Georgia 4
Marvin 4
Willie 4

BOONE
Betsie H 41
BOWMAN
Alva R 4
Bernice N 4
BRACKETT
Ader 5
Alvie 5
Arvie 4
Ben 4
Beulah 4
Buran 4
Carrie 4
Charlies 4
Clyde 5
Dessie 5
Earl 4
Emily J 4
Evie 4
Fannie 4
Floyd 4
Henry 5
Horace 4
Howard 4
James 4
James B 4
James E 4
James K P 4
Jennie 4
Jesse 4
Jesse M 4
Jewel 4
John 4
John W 4
Junie 4
Lillie D 5
Martha M 4
Merica 4
Nannie L 5
Nettie L 4
Nola 4
Olie 4
Oscar J 4
Patrick 4

53

Index

Richard 4
Robert Lee 4
Roy 5
Savilla 5
Thomas B 5
Thomas C 5
Will 4
William B 5
Willie 5

BRADLEY
Annie 5
Dinah 5
Eliza Jane 5
Eoy 5
George 5
Henry 5
Henry T D 5
James 5, 24
James W 5
Johnson 41
Joseph 5
Judson W 5
Lidda 5
Lizzie 5
Maggie 5
Margaret M 5
Minda 5
Mindy A 5
Morgan 5
Nancy 5
Nick 5
Sarah 5
Vandalia 5
William Amos 5

BRADY
Arthur 41
Eliza 41
Elizabeth 41
Luther 41
McKinley 41
Robert A 41
Sarah 41

BRAY
Jesse 41

Nellie 41
BROOKS
Mollie 5
BROWN
Daniel 5
Daniel A 5
Elmer 5
Eva 5
Georgia 5
Harry L 5
Howard Jerome 5
James V 5
Jennie 5
Jessie M 5
Jonas 5
Katie L 5
Luke 5
Lydia 5
Mark 5
Mary C 5
Mary Ethel 5
Oliver 5
Ora L 5
Pearl 5
Peter 5
Rogers Dixon 5
BRUCE
Essie 5
Eva 5
Frank 5
Harvey 5
Ida 5
Kissie E 5
Thomas 5
BRUNNETT
Lela 5
Sidie 5
Willie 5
BRYANT
Elizabeth H 5
BRYSON
Edna 5
Lena 5
BUCHANAN

Index

Mary E 18
BUNCH
  Carrie L 5
  Matison 5
  Morris 5
  Myrtle 5
  Nancy E 5
BURDETTE
  Burilla P 41
BURGESS
  Arthur 41
  Bessie L 5
  Bob Floy 5
  George A 5
  Georgia Sneed 5
  James 41
  John 41
  Martha 41
  Mary 41
  Mary M 5
  Olie 41
  Van 41
  Will Rose 5
BURNETT
  Martha E 5
BURNS
  Henewee 41
  Jack 41
  Marie 41
BUSHYHEAD
  Ben 6
  Nancy 6
BYRD
  Leona 41

CALHOUN
  Eve 6
  Godoquoskie 6
  Henry 6
  Lawrence 6
  Lloyd 6
  Morgan 6
  Sallie 6
  Wattie 6

  Yenkeenee 6
CALLOHOUN
  Joe 6
  Lawyer 6
  Ollie 6
CAMP
  Jas R 6
CAMPBELL
  Lurita 41
CANOUT
  Lizzie 6
  Maggie 6
CARTER
  Margaret L 6
  Martha A 6
  William H 6
CAT
  Bettie 6
  Jesse 6
  Johnson 6
  Lucy 6
  Mandy 6
  Margaret 6
  Sally 6
  Willie 6
CATE
  Elizabeth 6
CATOLST
  Charley 6
  Elec 6
  Eliza Jane 6
  Eve 6
  Jim 6
  Nancy 6
  Sallie 6
  Tamar 6
  Wallace 6
  William 6
CATT
  Sallie 6, 16
CAYLOR
  Mattie E 6
  Nancy E 6
  Sidney C 6

William L 6
CEARLEY
   Emory 6
   Lucie 6
   Luther 6
   Robert 6
CHADWI8CK
   Margaret M 41
CHADWICK
   Delia 41
   Margaret M 41
   Ruby 41
   William E 41
CHAMBERS
   Rosa M 6
   William A, Jr 6
CHANDLER
   William P 46
CHARLTON
   Catherine H 6
   Emily W 6
   Sallie Waters 6
   Thomas J 6
   Wilhelmina H 6
CHASTAIN
   Mary 6
   William B 6
   Wrenie F 6
CHATMAN
   Artie 6
   Martha R 6
   Oscar 6
   Thomas 6
CHE-WO-NA 6
CHICKALALA
   Andy 6
CHICKALEELAH
   Annie 6
   John 6
CHICKILULA
   Jacob 6
   Loosy 6
   Mary 6
   Sowanu 6

Stone 6
CHILDASKI
   Charlotte 6
   Queta 6
   Waddie 6
   Will 6
CHILDERS
   Lula F 6
   Robert 6
   Walter 6
CHU-LO-AN-WE
   Fidel 6
CHU-LO-DA-DEGI
   Jimmie 6
CHURCH
   Mary B 6
CLAY
   Timpson 6
CLEMONT
   Barnie 7
   Callie 7
   Mary M 7
CLIFT
   Marie I 7
   Nellie D 7
   Robert B 7
   Walter D 7
CLIMBINGBEAR
   Ancy 7
   Daleeskee 7
   Katie 7
   Mabel 7
   Ollie 7
CLINGAN
   Cherokee L 7
   Edward E 7
   Elijah E 7
   William K 7
CLOUD
   Sallie 7
COCHRAN
   Arch 7
   Casey 7
   Dehkie 7

Index

Dorcus 7
James 7
COLDING
  Letitia F 7
COLE
  Arlie 7
  Enert 7
  Evert 7
  George W 7
  Ida 7
  Jewel 7
  John 7
  Laura 7
  Oma 7
  Robert 7
  Walter 7
  William 7
COLLAKE
  Ada 7
  Bettie J 7
  Crofford V 7
  James 7
  Ora M 7
  Robert E 7
  Thomas G 7
  William C 7
COLNESKEY
  Tom 7
CO-LO-NA-HAS-KIE
  Jesse 9
COLONAHESKI
  Abram 7
  Isiah 7
  Jesse 7
  Katie 21
  Mark 7
  Martha 7
  Nancy 21
COLONAH-HES-KIH
  Tom 7
COMPTON
  Ann S 7
  Ellen H 7
  Juliette C H 41

Juliette Ch 7
Juliette H 7
Mary K 7
Omelie B 7
Shelby S 7
CONCENE
  Jake 7
  Manuel 7
  Ona 7
  Ropetwister 7
CONLEY
  Dorah 7
  Jennie 7
  John 7
  John, Jr 7
  Luke 7
CONSEEN
  Auganiah 7
  Jack 7
  Kate 7
  Martha 7
  Quakee 7
  Sallie 7
  Sally 7
  Thompson 7
CONSEENE
  Dayunne 8
  Nancy 8
CONSENE
  Nancy 8
  Peter 8
CONSTANT
  Elizabeth 8
  John B 8
  Magnolia 8
CON-TEES-KEE 8
  Caroline 8
COOPER
  Allie D 41
  Arnold 8
  Catherine L 8
  Celia Bell 8
  Curdoas J 8
  Fannie G 8

Index

Frankey N 8
Fred W 8
Laura 8
Laura A 41
Mack 8, 38
Myrtle D 8
Raymond F 41
Stacy Jane 8
William G 41
CORN
  Elisha 8
  Eliza M 8
  Frank 8
  Mary M 8
CORNETT
  Ernest J 8
  Laura J 8
  Lora A 8
  Luler M 8
  Luther S 8
CORNSILK
  Annie 8
  Armstrong 8
  David 8
  Dow 8
  Emeline 8
  E-yah-ni 8
  Hattie 8
  Howard 8
  Johnnie 8
  Martha 8
  York 8
COWART
  Nita See 8
  Thomas 8
CRAIG
  Alice 8
  Arvel 8
  Frank 8
  Georgie 8
  John 8
  Joseph 8
  Mary 8
  Nadia 8

Robert D 8
Roy 8
Wiley 8
William 42
CRANE
  Maria 8
  Mary A 9
CRANMORE
  Amanda B 8
CROFT
  John Henry 8
  John Lester 8
  Joseph 8
  Joseph B 8
  Martha E 8
  Mary I 8
  Mary Lillie 8
  Minnie 8
  Sarah E 8
  William L 8
  Willie L, Jr 8
CROMWELL
  Margaret P 8
CROW
  Annie 8
  Arthur 9
  Boyd 8
  Callie 8
  Caroline 8
  David 8
  Dorg 9
  Etta 8
  Joe 8
  John 8
  Lossel 9
  Luther 9
  Mary L 8
  Minnie 8
  Nonie 29
  Ossie 8
  Robert 9
  Sallie 8
  Sam 8
  Ute 6

Index

Wesley 8, 9, 20, 31
Wesley R 9
Wesley S 9
CROW, ... 9
CROWDER
   Florence W 9
   Kelsio M 9
   Liaaie 9
   Sedder B 9
CUCUMBER
   Arch 9
   Ar-gum-too-ga 9
   Dorcas 9
   Gena 9
   Gun-to-gy 9
   Katy 9
   Lilly 9
   Mose 9
   Ollie 9
   Willie 9
CUNSEENE
   Breast 9
   Donnie 9
   Jim 9
   John 9
   Mary 9
   Willie 9
CUPP
   Pearl 9
   Willie C 9

DAH-LE-YE-SKEE
   Se-gil-lie 9
DALE
   John Thomas 9
   Willie 9
DARLAN
   Bessie 42
   Harriet 42
   Will Mc 42
DARNELL
   Eliza 9
DAVIS
   Alsie 10

Amanda 9
Annie 9
Anstell N 10
Arthur 9
Arvaline 42
Bevilla G 10
Caroline 10
Charley 9
Clara 9
Clarence 9
Clinton 9
Cynthia 9
Dahick 9
Dan C 9
Daniel 9
Daniel, Jr 9
David 9
Delilah J 9
Dock 9
Earl 9
Earl T 10
Earl, Jr 9
Frank 10
Geo A 9
George 9
Henley 10
Isaac 9
Israel 9
James G 10
Jefferson 10
Jesse E 9
Jetta A 10
Joe 9
John 9
John H 10
Julia 9
Kate L 10
Katy 9, 18
Kinney 9
Lafayette 9, 10
Lee 9
Lena 10
Lena L 10
Lila Mary 9

59

Index

Lillian 10
Lizzie 9
Lorenzo D, Jr 10
Lorenzo N 10
Luda 10
Mamie 9
Marion 42
Mary L 10
Mattie 9
Miller 9, 10
Nellie 9
Quattie 10
Rebecca 10
Rufe 9
Sallie S 10
Samuel L 10
Sarah Jane 9
Stewart 9
Susan 9
Thos J 10
William 10
William E 10
William J 10
Willie 9
Wilste 10

DAY
Mattie A 10

DEDAHLEEDOGEE
Anna 10
Annie 10
David 10
Jackson 10
Jim W 10
Johnson 10
Jona-ni 10
Sherman 10
Wilson 10

DEGE
Charles F 10

DICKAGTISKA
Sallie 10

DICKEN
Watson 10

DICKEY
Ettie 10
Nannie 10

DICKSON
James R 10
Maude 10
Myrtle 10
Savannah G 10
Stacy 10

DILLARD
Tennessee 27

DILLINGHAM
Bettie 10

DOBSON
John 10
Mary 10

DOCKERY
Eliza 10
Emma 10

DOCKINS
Tobitha 10

DOUGHERTY
Allie 10
Ben 10
Charles E 10
Hillard 10
Homer 10
John H 10
Lizzie 10
Lora 10
Polina 10
Romania 10
Seaborn 10
Susan J 10

DOWNING
Arch 10
Sally 10

DRIVER
Abraham 10
Acgeenee 11
Adam 11
Allie 10
Chickalee B 10
Dick 10
Eliza 11

Index

George 10
Goliath 11
James 11
John 11
Judas B 11
Lossil 11
Lucinda 11
Lucy 11
Marion 11
Nannie 10
Ned 11
Quattie 11
Rosa 10
Samuel 10
Wesley 11
Will 11
DUNCAN
Lillian V 11
Subal 11
DUNLAP
Alice 11
Berry 11
Mary A 42
Robert 11

EDMONDS
Emille 11
Pink 11
Robert 11
Thomas 11
ELLIOTT
Gracie 11
John 11
Stella Pearl 12
ELLISON
John 11
Minnie 11
ELMORE
Don 12
Sallie Ann 12
ENOLA
Don 11
ERVIN
Claud 11

Maggie 11
Willard 11
ETTER
Sarah V 11
EUBANKS
Martha L 3, 11
Roger Roy 11
EVANS
Bonnie 11
Elmer 11
Horner 11
Mary Ann 11
Tate 11
FAUCETT
Irene 11
Nancy 11
FEATHER
Annie 11
Ge-law-mi-je 11
Jonah 11
Lawyer 11
Mary 11
Nancy 11
FEATHERHEAD
Nancy 11
Wilson 11
FIELDS
John 11
FINGER
Leona A 11
Ramona I 11
Samuel A 11
Sophria C 11
FOSTER
Alcy 11
Butson 11
Lee Roy 11
Robert 11
FREELAND
Delia H 11, 13
Ida L 11, 13
Martha 13
Martha C 11

Index

William H 11, 13
FRENCH
  Awee S 11
  Charlotte 12
  Ella Nona 12
  George B 11
  Jesse 12
  Maggie 12
  Maronie 11
  Maud 11
  Morgan 11
  Ned 12
  Nellie Maria 12
  Ross 12, 34
  Soggie 11
  Wallie 12

GANN
  Allen 12
  Gertie 12
  Henry 12
  James R 12
  Raymond 12
  Robert A 12
  Robert R 12
  William T 12

GARLAND
  Addie 12
  Elizabeth 12
  Emery 12
  Jesse T 12
  Jessie M 12
  John B 12
  Lonza 12
  Rodie 12
  Rozanna 12
  Tullis B 12
  William S 12

GARMONY
  Jane S 12

GARRARD
  Eliza A 12
  James W 12
  John E 12

Mary E 12
GARRETT
  Calvin 12
  Dovey 12
  Lou 12
  Mary 12
  Ola 12
  Van 12

GASPARETTI
  Catharine 12
  Johnny 12
  Mary Ann 12
  Raphael 12
  Thomas 12
  Victor 12

GASTON
  Allie 12
  Charles 12
  Martha 12
  T L 12

GEARING
  Eliza 12

GEORGE
  Agnes 12
  Alsie 12
  Alsie Bearmeat 12
  Annie 12
  Cain 12
  Celie 12
  Charlotte B 12
  Davis 12
  Dawson 12
  Elijah 12
  Ester 13
  Green 12
  Jackson 12
  Jacob 12
  Joe Stone 12
  Judas 12
  Julia V 12
  Lewis 12
  Lindy 12
  Lizer 12
  Lizzie 12

Index

Logan 12
Manly 12
Mark 12
Martha 12
Mary 12
Nancy 12
Ollie 12
Quatie 12
Shell 13
Shon 13
Suttawage 13
Yonaskin 12
GIBBONS
Cordelia 13
GILL
Calsina 13, 42
Charlie 42
Ludie 42
Noah 42
Robbie 42
Shelly 42
GILLESPIE
Grace 13
James R 13
John W 13
Marcus E 13
Tennessee 13
William R 13
GOBLE
Arvek 13
Benjamin 13
Bert 13
Colquitt 13
Duncan 13
Earl 13
Emma 13
George W 13
Harley 13
Harvey 13
Henry 13
Hershal 13
James 13, 46
James L 13
John 13

John W 13
Joseph 13
July 13
Lee 13
Leonard 13
Liza 13
Louis 13
Louvina 13
Madelphia 13
May 13
Mollie 13
Nancy 13
GOFORTH
Minnie 13
GOINS
Ban 13
Henry 13
James 13
GOINSNAKE
Nancy 13
Stephen 13
GOLECH
Maggie 13
GOSS
Amy 13
Bennie K 13
Bonnie Lynn 13
Clarice E 13
Ernest 13
Ethel A 13
Lella M 13
GOSSETT
Albert 13
Ardealy 13
Earnest 13
Harry 13
Lena 13
Mary 13
Viola 13
William 13
GRASSHOPPER 44
Jarett 13
Jarrett 36
Will 13

GRAVITT
  Brite 13
  Carrie 13
  Cora 13
  Emma 13
  George W 13
  Hallie 13
  James 13
  John 13
  Lester 13
  Lolie 13
  Norris 13
  Oconel 13
  Pearl 13
  Pollie 13
  Susie 13
  Thomas 13
  Willie 13

GRAYBEARD
  Ezekial 13
  James 14
  Lillie 13
  Sallie 14
  Stacy 14

GREEN
  Andrew 14
  Cora Elizabeth 14
  Henry 14
  Minnie B 14
  Thomas 14

GREYBEARD
  Aggie 14

GRIFFITH
  Addie 14

HAGGARD
  Mary F 42
  Myrtle G 42
  Nellie M 42
  Sandle T 42

HAIL
  David W 14
  John F 14
  Kittie 14

  Ninnie 14

HALL
  Ethel Eveline 14

HAMILTON
  Lizzie 14
  Martha 14
  Myrtle 14

HANCOCK
  Donald C 14
  Glennis R 14
  Ralph J 14
  Sallie E 14
  Sarah J 14

HANKINS
  Daisey 15

HANNAH
  Alva Reter 14
  Beulah H 14
  Dave F 14
  Jack W 14
  James E 14
  James M 14
  Jas M 14
  Jessie Lee 14
  Joseph Columbus 14
  Marvin M 14
  Mary Cecil 14
  Mary White 14
  Pauline M 14
  Sophia Lee 14
  Wallace P 14

HARALSON
  Susan D 14

HARDIN
  Anna E 14
  Arnis E 14
  Belvia A L 14
  Cain 14
  Celia 14
  Charles H 14
  Dillard 14
  Dock 14
  Dolphus 14
  Frank J 14

Grant 14
Hardie 14
Hubbard 14
James O 14
James W 14
Lillian M 14
Lousine 14
Loyd 14
Mattie 14
Oden 14
Pearley 14
Richard S 14
Romelus 14
Roy 14
Sattie 14
Thomas J 14
Verdia E 14
Virge 14
William H 14
William J 14
Willie P 14
HARMAN
Ellen C 14
George L, Jr 14
Julie C 14
HARRIS
Benjamin H 14
Bertha 14
George W 42
John A 42
John E 42
Mary L 42
Mindo Black ... 14
Ollie 14
Raymond 14
Romeo 14
HARTNESS
Julia 42
HAWKINS
Charles 15
Dora 15
HAYGOOD
Carrie 42
HENRY

Hubert P 15
Hugh B 15
Joseph J 15
Robert G 15
HENSLEY
Arthur 15
Arthur J 15
Claud 15
Ellen Lena 15
Emma 15
Emma Jane 15
Estela May 15
Grace P 15
Ida M 15
J V 15
James Robert ... 15
John Luther 15
Mary J 15
Nora 15
HENSON
Mary A 15
HIGGINS
Berney B 15
Georgia V M ... 15
Gracy 15
Lavina 15
Lee 15
Nellie P 15
Noah 15
Nylus 15
Ollie 15
Starling 15
Starling V 15
Zollie 15
HILDEBRAND
Amelia E 15
Eliza Jane 15
John W 15
Lawrence 15
Lawrence W, Jr ... 15
Lawrence, 3rd ... 15
HILL
Abraham 15
Ann 15

Index

Annie 15	Johnson 16
Blaine 15	Jules 15
Caroline 15	Lewis 16
Gudger G 15	Maggie 16
Hausley 15	Malissa 15
Henrietta C 15	Martha 15
John 15	Olive Ann 15
Kelley 15	Ollie 15
Levi 15	Rebecca 16
Maul 15	William 16
Moda Black 15	Wilson 16
Nancy 15	**HOUK**
Ned 15	Benson 16
Oden C 15	Carl 16
Sallie 15	Cormitha 16
Soggy M 15	Dorsey 16
HIX	Lillie 16
Sarah 15	Manerva 16
HOLLAND	**HOWELL**
Jennie S 15	Bessy 16
HOLLINGSWORTH	Callie M 16
Iley A 15	Charles Henry 16
HOPKINS	Ellen E 16
Mary M 15	Emily C 16
HORNBUCKLE	Emily Collier 16
Addie 16	Emily K 16
Alice May 15	Emily Kate 16
Andy 16	Ernest G 16
Artie 42	Eston E 16
Ben 16	Evan C 16
Caroline 16	Frank R 16
Davis 15	Herbert T 16
Donny 15	James Cleland 16
Dora 16	Joseph B 16
Elvira 15	Julia B 16
Fred 16	Lee 16
George 15	Letitia Pooler 16
Hartman 15	Loranzie 16
Henry 15	Lucy 16
Israel 15	Luther 4, 16
Jefferson 15	Mary Davis 16
John 15	Mary Elizabeth 16
John Lewis 16	Ralph 16
John Russell 15	Robert El 16

Samuel M 16
Samuel W 16
Stephen Elliott 16
Thomas C 16
William 16
William D P 16
HUDSON
  Ellen S L 42
  Thomas Charlton 42
HUGGINS
  John H 16
  Julia A 16
  Lizzie 16
  Martha A 16
  Sarah N 16
HUGHES
  Clarence W 16
  Courtney C 16
  Eliza A 16
  Fanny M 16
  Gladys M 16
  Horace C 16
  Laura L 16
  Robert A 16
HULSEY
  Charley M 16
  Conrad L 16
  Lena 16
  Sarah 16
  Sarah Isabel 16
  William R 17
HUSLEY
  Alvin Alonzo 16
  Andrew Carl 16
  Annie Maud 16
  Henry Allen 16
  John Priestly 16
HYDEN
  Emma L 17
IKE
  Sam 17
ISBILL
  Isabell 17

Lillie M 17
Mary I 17
Sarah A 17
JACK
  Dais W 23
  Nancy 17
JACKSON
  Caroline 17
  Dakie 17
  David 17
  Edward 17
  Ella 17
  Florence 17
  Fox Squirrel 17
  Jack 4, 17
  Jacob 17
  John 17
  Jonas 17
  Lawyer 17
  Ollie 17, 44
  Robert 17
  Sarah 17
  Stacy 17
  Takie 17
  Wesley 17
JAMES
  Allen 42
  Asa 42
JENKINS
  Marcoda 17
JESSANN
  Sim De Hart 17
JESSANNIH
  Lydia 30
JESSON
  Joe 17
  John 42
  Lydia J 17
JOEREE
  Dahonala J 17
  Mary 17
JOHNERIWAYNE 17
JOHNSON

Index

Addison 17
Anna R 17, 38
Caroline 17
Charlie M 17
China 17
Cider 17
Dora 17
Go-lin-die 17
Isaac 42
James 12, 17
James N 17, 38
Jennie 17
Kimpsie 17
Lunchi 17
Richard C 17, 38
Simon 12
Skeeg 17
Stephen 17
Tempa 42
Thomas C 17, 38
Yona 17
JO-LA-OO-GO-OOTH
Amy 17
JONES
Annie C 18
JORDAN
Felix R 46
Mollie 46
JOREE
Jessan 18
Joe 18
Lydia 18
JUMPER
Betsy 18
Edward 18
Ella 18
James 18
Stancie 18
Thomas 18
Ute 18
JUNULUSKIE 18

KANOUGHT
Abel 18

Columbus 18
KEG
James 18
Katie 18
KEGG
Modiah 18
KELL
Alexander 18
Andy 18
Arthur B 18
Bryson 18
Effa 18
Florida 18
Ida 18
Lucinda 18
Oran 18
Richard 18
Susanna 18
KEY
Laney C 18
Samantha 18
William C 18
KEYS
Reed M 18
Texas C 18
William S 18
Willie Maud 18
KIDD
David 18
De 18
Luther 18
Walter 18
Wesley 18
William 18
KILLGORE
Eula 42
Eulalie 42
Lena 42
KIRBY
Margaret 18
William 18
KIRKLAND
Georgia E 18
Martha L 18

Index

KIRKSEY
- Alvin M 42
- Eugene 42
- Fanny 42
- Florence M 42
- George B M 42
- Isabella 42
- Jewell M 42
- Mary 42
- Mattie 42
- Reuben L 42
- William W 42

KNOUGHT
- Sonsey 18

KRIGBAUM
- James A 46

LAMBERT
- Albert 18
- Albert J 18
- Alice R L 18
- Andrew 18
- Bessie A 18
- Capter Moses 18
- Charles Jackson 18
- Charley 18
- Clauda 19
- Cora Lee 19
- Corbett 19
- Edward 18
- Finley 18
- Fritz Simmes 18
- George Fred 18
- Georgia 18
- Herman 19
- Hugh 18
- Hugh H 18
- Hugh N 18
- Isaac 18
- Jack 18
- Jackson 18
- James M 18
- James W 18
- Jesse James 18
- Jessie 18
- John 19
- John N 18
- Joseph 19
- Julia F 19
- Katherine 45
- Lee F 18
- Lo9yd 18
- Lula 18
- Luzena 18
- Mary 18
- Minnie Hester 18
- Nannie G 19
- Ollianna 18
- Pearley 18
- Pierson 18
- Roscoe 18
- Sallie 18, 34
- Samuel 19
- Theodora R 19
- Thomas 19
- Thomas R 19
- Tilden 19
- Verdie 19
- William 18
- William H 18

LANCE
- Ira D 19
- John M 19
- Joseph M 19
- Mary E 19
- Mary V 19
- Thomas J 19

LANE
- Clark 13

LANGLEY
- Alfred A 19
- Amanda 19
- Ann 19
- Augustus 19
- Charles 19
- Chesley 19
- Columbus C 19
- Della 19

Index

Elma 19
Essie 19
Eulana J 19
Frank C 42
George 19
Josephine 19
Lilley May 19
Lizzie 19
Mary M 19
Matie 19
Mauda Lee 19
May 19
Minnie Lee 42
Missa 19
Mollie 19
Nora Dell 19
Robert 19
Sarah 19
Vinia 19
Walter 19
Warren M 19
Wheeler 19
William 19
William A 19
William T 19
LANGSTON
   Bessie F 19
   Dixie Lee 19
   Esther L 19
   Ollie M 19
   Rosa Lee 19
   Walter F 19
   William A 19
LARCHEE
   Daniel 19
LASSY
   Annie 20
   Leander 20
LAWRENCE
   Chas Colding 19
LAWSON
   Charlie 19
   Dave L 19
   Hayes 19

Jennie 19
Johnyasie 19
Kannada 19
Leandy 19
Thompson 19
LEADFORD
   Adkins 19
   Catherine M 19
   Cora 19
   Iowa 19
   Minnie 19
LEATHERWOOD
   Addie 19
   Coreine G 19
   Lela 19
   Luther 19
LEDFORD
   Allenie 19
   Annie 19
   Charley 19
   Eave 19
   Jacke 19
   Joe 19
   John 19
   Kiney 19
   Lucyan 19
   Mary 19
   Moses 19
   Polly 42
   Riley 19
   Sampson 19
LEE
   Alice M 19
   Alonzo 19
   Debrader 19
   Edith 19
   Laura Ann 19
   Oberlander 19
   Samuel 19
LEFEVERS
   Linnie 19
   Temoxyenah 19
   William E 19
LEMINGS

Index

Nannie 19
Ollie 19
LENOIR
   Annie 19
   Daisy 19
   Edgar 19
   Henry Clifton 19
   John Alber 19
   Lula 19
   Mamie 19
   May 19
   Mrs J M 19
   Thomas R 19
LEWIS
   Christine 20
   Estelle 20
   Fred N 20
   Henry W 20
   Irene 20
   James W 20
   John E 20
   Mable E 20
   Maley 20
   Myrtle 20
   Thomas A 20
LITTLE JOHN
   Elowih 42
   Goo-lah-gee 42
   Sally Anne 42
   Sow-wah-nee 42
LITTLEJOHN
   Annie 20, 38, 39
   Annie E 20
   Elowih 20
   Garrett 20
   Gion 20
   Henson 20
   Ike 20
   Isaac 20
   John 20
   Kate 20
   Mary 20, 33
   Mindy 20
   Owen 20

Sallie 20
Sounooke 20
Twister 20
Wiggins 20
Will 20
LOCUST
   John 20
   Lomie B 20
   Louis McK 20
   Nellie 20
   Noah 20
   Peter 20
   Polly Ann 20
   Tennie R 20
   Tiney 20
   Will 20
LONG
   Adam 20
   Aggie 20
   Bettie 20
   Cah-we-li 20
   Charley 20
   Da-gi-ni 20
   Dobson 20
   Ella 20
   Elsie 20
   Emeline 20
   Eve 20
   Garlonuskie 20
   Isaac 20
   Jackson 20
   Joe 20
   John 20
   John W 20
   Johnson 20
   Lee-wih 20
   Lizzie 20
   Long B 20
   Lucy 20
   Lucy Ann 20
   Maggie 20
   Maggie W 20
   Nola 20
   Peter 20

Index

Polly 20
Rachel 42
Sallie 20
Scott 20
Willie W 20
Wilson 20
LOOSEY
Henry 20
Solomon 20
LOSSIE
Agie 20
Dobson 20
John 20
Lloyd 20
Nancy 20
Nicer 20
LOUDERMILK
Beckey 20
Cora 21
Cynthia 20
Elmer 21
Hollie 20
John 20
Josephine 21
Luther 20
Nora 21
Rosey 20
LOW
John J 21, 43
Mary Rogers 43
LOWEN
John 21
John B 21
Sis 21
LOWERY
Andrew 46
Elsie J 46
Henry C 46
Susie 46
LUNSFORD
Callie 21
Daisy 21
LYNCH
Nancy E 46

MABRY
Sallie B 46
MCALISTER
Harriet C 21
MCCLANAHAN
Earl 21
Nellie 21
Ona 21
MCCOY
Bessie 21
David 21
Eliza M 21
James 21
James D 21
James M 21
James W 21
John M 21
John T 21
Julia 21
Marinda 21
Mary 21
Pearson 21
Stella 21
Stella May 21
William T 21
MCDANIEL
John D 21
Lulie E 21
MCDONALD
Addie 43
Andy 43
Belva 21
Catherine 21
Ethel 21
Grace 21
Harrison 21
Hobert 43
James 43
John, Jr 43
Loyd 43
Mack 42, 43
Mamie S 21
Mary 2, 21

May 43
Myrtle 43
Robert 42, 43
Walter 43
West 43
MCDOUGAL
   Estes 21
   Hershel 21
   Lorena 21
   Samantha 21
MCELREATH
   Andrew 21
   Charley 21
   Flora 21
   Floyd 21
   Fred 21
   India May 21
   Jennie May 21
   Lewis W 21
   Mary A 21
   Melly 21
   Sarah C 21
MCGEE
   Sarah L 21
MCKINLEY
   Ross 20
MCLEMORE
   Albert 21
   Claud 21
   Cora May 21
   Dorothy 21
   Emer 21
   Esther Ann 21
   Fannie M 21
   Frankie 21
   John W 21
   Mary 21
   Morell 21
   Morell M 21
   Samuel H 21
   Samuel Ros 21
   William L 21
MCSPADDEN
   Faith H 21

Walter 21
MALICOATE
   Laura 31
MANEY
   Cordela 21
   Eve Wilnoty 43
   Flora B 21
   John 43
   Mary 43
   Minnie A 21
MANING
   Maimi Ethel 12
MARTIN
   Angeline 21
   Daliskee 21
   David Lee 22
   Edith M 43
   Essie 21
   Ester Janie 22
   Frances 22
   George 22
   Gurley 22
   Hubert M 43
   James G 22, 43
   Kate 22
   Lenar 22
   Lucy 22
   Paul H 43
   Smith A 22
   Suate 22
   Thomas 22
   Thomas E 22
   Van B 22
   Wesley L 22
   William W 22, 43
MASHBURN
   Bertha 22, 43
   Bessie 22
   Florence 43
   Frank 22
   Harriett A 22
   James L 22
   Kate 43
   Leora 22

Mattie 22
Minnie 22
Norma 43
Sarah A 22
Susan 43
MATHEWS
  Evie 22
  Lillie 22
MEADOWS
  David T 22
  Elizabeth 22
  John G 22
  Mary J 22
MEE
  Katie Van 43
  Katie Vann 22
MERONEY
  Bailey 22
  Bailey B 22
  Bessie 22
  Della 22
  Felix P 22
  Fred 22
  Gertrude 22
  John S, Jr 22
  Lula 22
  Margaret A 22
  Martha A 22
  Mays 22
  Richard B 22
  Sllie B 22
  William H 22
MERRELL
  Albert II 22
  John 22
  Ransey 22
MICHAELS
  Eliza 22
MILLER
  Carl 22
  Flonnie A 43
MIMS
  Cora L 22
  David Ross 22

  Ella M 22
  Margaret I 22
  Robert A 22
  William P 22
MINK
  Nes-see 22
MONDY
  Maud 22
  Vera 22
MONEY
  Hazeltine 14
MONROE
  Nora A 22
MOON
  Aaron 22
  Abner L 22
  Benjamin 22
  Callie 22
  Nellie 22
  Thomas 22
  Wm N 22
MOOR
  Cynthia A 22
  Elizabeth B 22
  John Frederick 22
  Lottie 22
  Sarah A 22
  Sarah L 22
  Wm Clifton 22
MOORE
  Celia 23
  Malvin 23
MORGAN
  Orange 43
MORRISON
  Beula 23
  Blanche 23
  Della 43
  Eddie 43
  Fred 23, 43
  Jessie 23
  Myrtle 43
  Ollie 23
  Patty Edgar 43

Index

MUMBLEHEAD
- Charles C 23
- Elizabeth 23
- James B 23
- John D 23
- Rodgers L 23
- Rosey Bell 23
- Tawney 43

MURPHY
- Arch 23
- David 43
- Howard 43
- Isabella 43
- Jane 43
- Jesse 23
- Joe 43
- Leander 28, 43
- Lillia Arch 23
- Louisa 43
- Lucy A 18
- Manco 43
- Mandie 43
- Maneve 43
- Margaret 43
- Martin 43
- Mary 23
- Sollie 43
- Walter 43
- Willard 43
- William 23

NED
- Annie 23
- Ezekiel 23
- Julie 23

NEGOOJAGE
- Ann Elizie 23
- James 23
- Lidge W 23
- Maggie 23
- Mark 23
- Ollie 23

NES-SEE
- Mink 22

NEWTON
- Bettie 23
- Eva M 23
- James 23
- John 23
- Lestr 23
- Pearl 23

NICHOLS
- Octavia N 23
- Pryor O 23
- Taylor O 23

NICK
- Wesley C 23

NIGAJACK
- Lucinda 23
- Moses 23
- Nancy 23

NOTTYTOM
- Nancy 23
- Peter 23

ODOM
- Addie D 23
- Biddie D 23
- Cicero 23
- Garland 23
- Loy Felton 23

OH-LEE-HEE-NEE 23

OKWATAGA
- Elizabeth 23

OLIVER
- Beulah 23
- Estie 23
- Ida 23
- Lucinda 23
- Mary L 23

O'NEAL
- Beulah C E 23
- Conrad 23
- Eliza C E 23
- Laura 23
- Laura L 23
- Minnie M 23
- Wilburn K 23

Index

William E P 23
OO-CUMMA
  Aleck 23
  Annie 23
  Enoch 23
  Esther 23
  James 23
  Jennie 23
  Wilson 23
OO-DAH-YIH 24
OOKUMMA
  Annie 43
OO-SOWIE
  Annie 24
  Jennie 24
  John 24
  Nicie 24
  Olise 24
  Olsie 24
  Olsinnih 24
  Paul 24
  Rachel 24
  Sallie 24
  Sam 24
  Shell 24
  Susie 24
  Tah-quette 24
  Willie 24
OO-TAHL-KEE
  Quakee 24
OSKIN-NEE 24
OSKISON
  Helen Day 24
  John, Jr 24
OTTER
  Allen 43
  Andrew 24
  Elizabeth 24
  Jackson 24
  Lindia 24
  Matilda 24
  Nancy 24
  Ollick 24
  Ollie 24
  Sallie 24
  Sarah 24
  Wilson 24
  Winnie 24
OWEN
  Isabell McD 43
OWL
  Adam 24
  Agner 24
  Allen 24
  Amons 24
  Annie 24
  Betsy 24
  Blue 24
  Bryan 24
  Callie 24
  Cornelia T 24
  Cornelious 24
  David 24
  Davis 24
  Dinah 24
  Dora 24
  Enoch 24
  Etha 24
  Freal Mc 24
  George A 24
  Henry P 24
  James 24
  Jane 24
  John 24
  Johnson 24
  Jonah 24
  Lloyd 24
  Lula 24
  Mandy 44
  Margaret 24
  Mark 24
  Martha 24
  Mose 24
  Quety 24
  Quincy 24
  Sampson 24
  Samuel 24
  So-kin-ni 24

Index

Solomon 24
Stacy 24
Suate 24
Tahquette 44
Theodore 24
Thomas 24
Thomas W S 24
William 24

PADGETT
Ada C 24
Artie W 24
Isabella J 24
Mary M 24
Nellie Dimma ... 24
PALMOUR
Myrtle K 24
PANKEY
Dessie May 24
Elanora 24
Marvin 24
PANTHER
Bessie 24
Goliath 24
Job 24
John 24
Mark 24
Nancy 24
PARKER
Aaron 25
Caroline 25
Colquit 44
Josie 25
Julian 25
Paul 25
Roxey 44
Taylor 44
William 44
PARRIS
Catharine 25
Laura May 25
PARTRIDGE
Mose 25
Nelly 25

Sallie 25
Winnie E 25
PASCHAL
Geo Walter 25
Walter 25
PASSMORE
Cardie 25
A L 25
Nancy J 25
Thomas 25
PATTERSON
Arvis 25
Celie 25
Elizabeth 25
Ella 25
Elmer 25
Ethel 25
Hobert 25
Iowa 44
Josie 44
Lula 25
Lura 44
Olden 25
Onzo 25
PAYNE
Ada 25
Albert F 25
Betty 25
David L 25
Duke 25
Elisha 25
Ellen 25
Emma O L 25
Ephraim 25
Felix 25
Grace L 25
Hazel 25
James M 25
Jim 25
John 25
Louise 25
Lucy 25
Lydia M 25
Mack 25

77

Mary Jane 25
Oliver 25
Polly E 25
Rollen T 25
Sally 25
Thomas 25
William A 25
William E 25
PENDLETON
Walter 6, 25
PERKINS
Burt 25
Georgia 25
Gordon 25
PERRY
George M 25
Julia B 25
Julia D 25
Mamie 25
Watson 25
William C 25
PHEASANT
Dora 25
John 25
Waggie 25
William 25
PHILYAW
Dewey 44
Enner 44
Jennie 44
PINSON
Bertha 25
Clara 25
Eula 25
Guy 25
POPE
Allen 25
Allie T 25
Aora 25
Blaine 25
Elisia L 25
Harley 25
James 25
Lizzie L 25

Martha 25
Mary H 25
Maybell 25
Thomas L 25
William F L 25
PORTER
Florence S 25
Iris 25
James D 25
Tommy 25
POTTER
Tommy 11
POWELL
Doogah 26
Frank E 26
Gober 26
Holmes 26
James E 26
John A 26
John C 26
Mose 26
Moses 26
Sadie 26
Sarah 26
Stancel 26
Stansell 26
Took 26
Vernon 26
William 26
Winnie 26
PUCKETT
Ella 44
George 44
Lula May 44
Roy 44
PULLIUM
Caroline 26
Decatur 26
Elizabeth 26
Galusha 26
PURYEAR
Frank M 26
Hamp Y 26
Mary A 26

Index

QUAIN
   Walter 26
   Wodesutta 26
QUARLES
   Bearl G 26
   Charley 26
   Henry B 26
   Henry G 26
   James D 26
   Luther 26
   Mary A 26
   Mary B 26
   Rosy B 26
   Roxie A 26
QUEEN
   Abraham 26
   Bessie 26
   Etta 26
   Jasper 26
   Levi 26
   Lucindy 26
   Malinda 26
   Mary 26
   Mindy 26
   Nolie 26
   Ollie 26
   Sallie 26
   Simpson 26

RACKLEY 26
RAINEY
   Annie Catherine 26
   Homer 26
   Janie 26
RALSTON
   Lucy 26
   Luke 26
   Violet 26
RANDOLPH
   Letitia M L 26
RAPER
   Alexander 26
   Alven 27

   Alvin 26
   Charles B 26
   Claud H 26
   Claude 27
   Clay 26
   Cli 27
   Clifton 27
   Clinton 27
   Dathney 27
   Delia 26
   Deltia C 26
   Denver Lee 26
   Dessie 26
   Dovie 26
   Edger 27
   Effie 27
   Elisha 26
   Elizie 26
   Emory 26
   Ever 27
   Gano 26
   George W 26
   Georgia Ann 26
   Girley 27
   Gracie 26
   Guss 27
   Harley T 26
   Harvey L 26
   Hency C 26
   Homer 26
   Iowa 26
   Iven 27
   Ivy Ann 26
   Jackson 26
   James 26, 27
   James B 26
   James C 26
   James T 26
   James, Jr 26
   Jerley 27
   Jesse Lafayette 27
   Jessie 27
   John H 27
   John Henry 27

Julia 27
Lillie May 27
Lizzie 27
Lon 26
Lou 27
Mamie 27
Manda 26
Margaret G 27
Marshal 27
Martin 27
Marty 27
Mary 26
Maudy Lu 26
Miran G 26
Naomie 27
Nathan 27
Pearl 26
Sam 27
Theodoosia 26
Thomas W 27
Verdy 27
Viola 27
Whoote 27
William 27
William B 27
William N 26
William T 27
Willie 27
RATLEY
Jim 27
Lucy 27
RATLIFF 26
Emma 27
Jacob 27
Lizzie 27
Loyd 27
William 27
RATTLER
Abie 27
Alucy 27
George 27
Henson 27
Morgan 27
Rachel 27

RAY
Alex W 27
Alexander W 27
Charles 29
Charles R 27
Fred J 27
Grace Gertrude 27
John F 27
John N 27
Lula Ella 27, 29
R D 27
Robert B 27
Vernon Dean 27
William 27, 29
REDFEARN
Jesse Dewitt 27
John Earl 27
Martha 27
REED
Dave 27
Fidille 27
Jesse 27
Lizzie 37
Lucy Ann 27
Maggie 27
Rachel 3, 27
Susan J 27
REID
[Eter 28
Adam 27
Cindy 28
Duweese 27
Irene 28
James 28
Jimmie 28
Johnson 27
Lloyd 28
Nannie 27
Noah 28
Rachel 27
Spade 28
Willie 28
Winnie 28
RICE

Index

Fannie 28
RICHARD
  Mamie 28
RING
  Charles H 28
  Ella N 28
  George W 28
ROBERSON
  Charley H 28
  Edward C 28
  Eleanor 28
  Ellen 28
  Emaline 28
  Fannie 28
  Ginty 28
  Gita 28
  Haddley 28
  James R 28
  Mary 28
  Sarah 28
  Willia 28
ROBERTS
  Charlotte 28
  Fred 28
  Walter 28
ROBERTSON
  Thomas 28
  William 28
ROBIN
  Richard 28, 38
ROBINSON
  Birgie 28
  Charles 28
  Willie 28
RODDY
  Elbert D 28
  Jessie R 28
  Leta M 28
  Ralph 28
RODGERS
  Cordelia 28
  George E 28
  Martha C 28
ROGERS

Aster 28
Augustus L 28
Boney 28
Clio A 28
Cordelia 44
Elizabeth 28
Ernest H 28
Ernest P 28
Floid 28
Florence S 28
Howard W 28
James C 28
Jeanette 28
John W 28
Julia E M 28
Louise E 28
Mamie E 44
Osker 28
Pearlie Ann 28
Raymond C 28
Robert C 28
Robert N 28
Ruth A 28
Viller 28
William 28
ROLLINGS
  Dovie 28
ROPETWISTER
  Annie 28
  Arneach 28
  John 28
ROSE
  Adam 29
  Annie 29
  Bonnie 29
  Buffalo Bill 29
  Carlie 29
  Florence 29
  Freeman 29
  Gracie 29
  Ida 29
  Jake 29
  Jennings 29
  Leslie 29

Index

Mandy 29
Myrtle 29
Nora 29
Rachel 29
ROSS
   Cain 29
   James 29
   Rosa 29
   William 29
RUDDLES
   Irena 29
RYAN
   Calvin 46
   Emmett 46
   William 46

SAKE
   Che-wah-nee 29
   Nellie 29
SA-LA-LU-SI
   Susannah 29
SA-LE-LEE-SI
   Susannah 35
SALOLANEETA 32
   Aggie 29
   Bird 29
   Henry 29
   Jessie J 29
   John 29
   John, Jr 29
   Jonas 29
   Laura 29
   Lindy 29
   Lizzie 29
   Lucy 29
SAMPSON
   James 29
   Sallie 29
SANDERS
   Julia 29
   Listy 29
   Mose 29
   Polly 29
SANFORD

Andrew H 29
Emily M 29
George H 29
James H 29
John H 29
Sarah M 29
William D 29
SATTERFIELD
   Amanda E 29
   Brilla D 29
   Henry T 29
SAUNOOKE
   Annie 44
SAWNOOKA 32
   Adam 29
   Amineeta 30
   Cindy 30
   Jackson 29
   James 29
   Jenny 29
   John 29, 30
   John, Jr 29
   Joseph 29
   Joseph A 30
   Josephine 29
   Malinda 29
   Margaret 29
   Nancy 29
   Nannie 29
   Nanny 30
   Ollie 29
   Osley B 30
   Polk 30
   Rachel 30
   Sallie 30
   Samuel 30
   Savannah 30
   Soggy 30
   Stacy 30
   Stephen E 30
   Stilwell 30
   Thompson 30
   Wal-lin-ny 30
   William 30

Windy 30
SAWYER
  Kiyini 30
  Thomas 30
SCALES
  Ann L 46
  George 46
  Grover 46
  Joseph 46
  Lillie 46
  Louisa 46
  Mary E 46
  Mattie 46
SCHICK
  John A 2
SCOTT
  Camble 30
SCREAMER
  Cain 30
  Cinda 30
  Enos 30
  James 30
  Manus 30
  Soggy 30
SEITZ
  Georgia A 30
  Henry G 30
  Jenny L 30
  Jenny Linn 30
  John C 30
SEQUOYAH 30
  Alice 30
  Amanda 30
  Jackalia 30
  Lizzie 30
  Louisa 30
  Luzena 30
  Noah 30
  Richard 30
  Running Wolf 30
  Suannah 30
  Tahquitte 30
SHADWICK
  Alice 30

  Clair 30
  Eddie Lonzo 30
  Ensola 30
  Ervin 30
  Manuel H 30
  Mary L 30
SHASTEEN
  Eliza E 30
  James W 30
  Lyman Lee 30
  Mary 30
  Nannie B 30
  Richmond S, Jr 30
  Roy H 30
  Sofrona E 30
  Thomas F 30
  Virginia E 30
  William B 30
SHED
  Harley R 30
  James G 30
  Martha J R 30
SHELL
  Alice 30
  Andy 30
  Bessie 30
  Hetty Feather 30
  Joe 30
  John 30
  Mattie 30
  Sally 30
  Ute 30
SHERRILL
  John Ute 30
  Julia 30
  Kinny 30
  Mollie 30
  Solomon 30
SILVER
  Edgar 30
  Emma 30
  Grady 30
  Victor 30
SITTON

Index

Emma 31
SIVLEY
   Caroline 31
   Claudie B 31
   Grocia Ann 31
   Jas D 31
   Joseph 31
   May 31
   Roy 31
SIXKILLER
   Jesse Martin 31
SKEE-KEE
   Jess 31
SKELLEY
   Charles 31
   Cora Belle 31
   Joseph 31
SKITTY
   Severe 31
SMITH
   Addie Lela 31
   Alice 44
   Amanda 20
   Arch 46
   Arizona 31
   Arthur 44
   Belva 44
   Bessie 31
   Beulah 31
   Blaine 44
   Callie 28, 31
   Calvin 31
   Carrie 31
   Charity 31
   Charley 31
   Charlie 31
   Cicero K 31
   Clea N 31
   Cynthia 31
   Daliah 31
   Dave 44
   Delilah 31
   Dell 31
   Duffie 31

Earl 32
Edgar 32
Elizabeth 31
Ellick 31
Emma 31
Emma C 31
Erskine Irene 31
Etta 31
Eula 31
Evelyn 31
Fanzy 31
Frances E 31
Garfield 44
George 31
George L 31
Gerald 32
Goldman 44
Gracie 32
Hartman 32
Henry 31
Henry H 31
Jacob 31
James 31
James D 31
James Harris 31
Jas F 22
Jesse 44
Jessie 31, 46
Joe 44
John 31
John C 32
John Henry 31
John Q 31
Josephine 31
Lee 46
Lester 44
Lewis H 31
Lizzie 31
Lloyd 31
Lorella 31
Lourainne 44
Mabel 31
Mamie 31
Mandie 31

Index

Mandy 46
Mark T 31
Marshall 31
Martha 31, 46
Mary 32
Mary Melvinie 44
Mattie 46
May 44
Minnie 31
Missouri 31
Myrtle 32
Nancy 31
Nellie 32
Noah 31
Olive Larch 31
Oliver 31
Robert 31
Robert E 31
Robson 31
Ross B 31
Rosy 31
Roxie 31
Russell 31
Sallie A 31
Sam 44
Samuel E 32
Stella 31
Susie 44
Sylena 31
Sylvester A 32
Teney 31
Thaddeus S 32
Thomas 32
Viola 31
Wallace J 31
Willie Clark 32
Willie May B 31
Winnie 31
SMOKER
Ahyoster 32
Awie 32
Axe Sam 32
Bascom 32
Charley 32

Cindy 32
Ganeleck 32
Jim 32
John 32
Kwous 32
Lizzie 32
Lloyd 32
Maggie 32
Olive 32
Os-kin-nee 32
Peter 32
Stacy 32
Will 32
SNEED
Annie 32
Campbell 32
John Harris 32
Manco 32
Mary 32
Maud 32
Osco 32
S B 32
Samuel 32
Sarah 32
Veco 32
William S 32
SNYDER
Susannah 32
SOL-EE-OL-EE-SEE
Waddie 32, 36
SOLOLANEETA
Annie 32
Leander 32
SOUNOOKE 32
SOWTHER
Dora 32
SPARKS
Belle 32
Carl 32
Harlie 32
Leroy 32
Sarah A 32
SQUIRREL
Awee 32

Daniel 32
David 32
Dinah 32
Fox 32
George 32
Kimsey 32
Mary 32
Nancy 32
Nora 32
Norah 32
Ollie 32
Quattie 32
Sarah 32
Sequtteh 32
STALLCUP
Nancy 32
STAMEY
Arch 32
James 32
Pearley 32
Winnie A 32
STANDINGDEER
Andy 32
Caroline 32
Junaluska 32
Lowin 32
Margaret 32, 33
Nana 33
Nancy 33
Wesley 33
STANDINGWATER
Aleck 33
Elsinnah 33
STANTON
Florence 33
STEWART
Arthur T 33
Celina K 46
Cordelia W 33
Dora 33
George W 46
John H 46
Levi 33
Lucinda 33

Max 46
William W 46
STILES
Alma 33
Clem 33
Emy 33
Floyd 33
Gilbert 33
Hal 33
Mary 33
Mary J 44
Minnie 33
Nina 44
Oliver 33
Omiu 44
Theodosia E 33
Thomas 44
Thomas Luster 33
Virgil 33
STONER
Thelma T 18, 33
Willie E 18, 33
STRICKLAND
Clifford A 33
Ellene 33
John Robert 33
Mary F 33
Roy 33
STULL
Missouri 33
SUATE
Martin 33
SU-DA-YU
Sallie Ann 21, 33
SULLINS
Paul S 33
SUMMEROUR
Ethel 33
Florence 33
Junia E 33
Katherine 33
Milton 33
Sam 33
SUTEGI 33

Mary 33
SUTER
   Charles W 33
   Diller... 33
   George 33
   John Riley.. 33
   Louvenia W 33
   Lueller 33
   Maggie... 33
   Martha 33
   Mary 33
SUTTON
   Nancy 33
SUWAGGIE
   Wadasutta 33
SWAYNEY
   Amanda 33
   Arizona 33
   Calle 33
   Frank.. 33
   Jesse... 33
   John W... 33
   Laura 33
   Lorenzo D 33
   Luzane 33
SWEANEY
   John T 46
SWIFT
   Benjamin W 33
   Frank B 33
   Mabel... 33
SWIMMER
   Annie 33
   John 44
   Louisa 46
   Lucian 33
   Mary 44
   Runaway 33
   Tom 33
TAHQUETTE
   Annie E.. 33
   Emily 33
   John A 33

TAH-QUIT
   Martha 33
TAH-YEH-YEH 33
TAIL
   Jim 34
TA-LA-LA
   Jackson 34
TA-LA-LA-
   John 34
TA-LA-LA
   Lucy 34
   McKinley...34
TA-LA-LA-
   Rebecca 34
TA-LA-LA
   Thomas..34
   Will..34
TATHAM
   Olive...34
   Stella..34
TAYLOR
   Bessie 34
   David 34
   Jack..34
   Jesse 34
   Jimmy..26
   John 34
   Julius 34
   Liza..34
   Maggie 34
   Olkinney..34
   Oo-la-i-way 34
   Rachel..34
   Sallie..34
   Sherman 34
   Stacy..34
   Temsey 34
   Thomas E 34
TEE-CEE-TES-KEE
   Arach..34
   Arawee 34
   Jessie 34
   Jonah 34
   Sallie..34

Index

TEETESKII
 Aggie 34
TE-KE-KE-SKI
 Celie 34
 Jesse.. 34
TESATEESKA
 John 34
 Lloyd 34
 Sampson 34
 Welch 34
TESATESKA
 Ella 34
 Mandy... 34
 Nancy 34
 Noah 34
 Will... 34
TESATESKY
 Eve.. 34
 Noah 34
THOMAS
 Alfred 34
 Allen R 34
 Allie A 34
 Annie J.. 34
 Bearl L 34
 Donor.. 44
 Ella Jane 34
 Harlin.. 34
 Herbert H 34
 Hiram L 34
 Jack S.. 34
 James A 34
 James H 34
 Joseph H 34
 A L 34
 Mandy... 34
 Pauline.. 44
 Sallie... 34
 Snow Belle 44
 Stella... 34
 Thomas Al 34
 William H 34
THOMASON
 Lissie I 34

 W B 34
THOMPSON
 Allison Garnett 34
 Arsene 34
 Atha...34
 E34
 Enis..34, 44
 Ernest 34
 Ernest Trice 34
 Goliath...44
 Greely..34
 Howard..34
 Hugh Chas.......................................34
 Iowa...34
 Iris 34
 Jewell 34
 Lydia 44
 Mandy 34
 Marion...34
 Martha...34
 Mary..34
 Mattie 34
 Minnie 34
 Nebraskey..34
 Olen...34
 Peter 44
 Vritis..34
 Wilson 44
THRASHER
 Claud 34
 Ella V 34
 Ethel 34
 Etta 34
 Flora 34
 Lee...34
 Myrtle..34
 Paul..34
 Thomas..34
TI-GOO-GI-DER
 Ka-lu-qua-ta-ke 35
TILLEY
 Oma...35
TIMPSON
 Callie May.......................................35

    Columbus H............................. 35
    James 35
    James A 35
    John S 35
    Umphrey P.............................. 35
TOHISKIE
    Going Bird 35
TOINEETA
    Arneach 35
    Caroline 35
    George 35
    Loney..................................... 35
    Martha 35
    Nick 35
    Quatie 35
    Sally....................................... 35
    Su-weg-ie............................... 35
    West....................................... 35
TOOMIE
    Andy 35
    Engeline................................. 35
    Isaac...................................... 35
    Joseph 35
    Mary 35
    Nancy 35
    Nannie 35
    Nick 35
TOONIE
    Legilly 42, 44
TOONIGH
    Anna 35
    Jukius.................................... 35
    Lige....................................... 35
    Mike 35
    Nancy 35
    Nicey 35
    Squency 35
TRAMPER
    Ammons 44
    Chiltoski 44
    Lottie 44
TREECE
    Daniel R................................. 35
    Ethel M.................................. 35

    Henry R 35
    Jessie A 35
    Mary E 35
    William D............................... 35
TREW
    Bigie R 35
    Calsina................................... 35
    Nora E 35
TROTT
    John R 35
    Johnnie 35
    Wm O 35
    Wm R 35
TROTTINGWOLF
    Annie..................................... 35
    Katie 35
    Moses 35
    Ned 29
TROTTINGWOLFE
    Ned 35
TUATLAY
    Nancy 34
TUCKER
    Dewey S 35
    James H 35
    James L 35
    John M................................... 35
    John W................................... 35
    Mary E 35
    Mary P 35
    William P 35
TURNER
    Bertha P................................. 35
    Clifford F............................... 35
    Emma Bell............................. 35
    James L 35
    John W 35
    Lidora A 35

UTE
    Andy 36

VAN
    Katie 36

Index

VEAL
- Charley 36
- Harley 36
- John 36
- Joseph 36
- Pratt 36
- Sarah L 36
- William 36

VICK
- Andy M 36
- Bessie 36
- Dessie 36
- Dora 36
- Lester 36
- Lockie 36
- Mary 36
- Sallie 36

VICTORY
- Andrew 47
- Anna A 47
- Charles 47
- Donney 47
- Samuel 47
- Susan 47
- Tensy 47

VOILES
- Annie M 36
- Bridy 36
- Cora 36
- Jane 36
- Jennie 36
- Jessie 36
- Vincent 36
- William 36

WADASUTTA
- Anna 33, 36

WADDIE
- Un-nigh 36

WADE
- Bird 36
- Davis 36
- Harold Clay 36
- Jos A 36

- Lee 36
- Nancy 36
- Stewart 36

WAGA
- Annie 36

WAH-CHECH-A
- Charley 36
- Jack 36
- Jarrett 36
- Jess 36
- Jim 44
- John W 36
- Nancy 36
- Onee 36
- Posey 36
- Quelick 36
- Roxie 36
- Sarah 36
- Susie 36
- Winnie 36

WAHHANEETA
- Allen 36
- Caroline 36
- John 36
- Maggie 36
- Posie 36
- Sallie 36
- Samson 36
- Samuel 36
- William 36

WA-HOO
- Elsie 11, 36

WAIHOO
- Caroline 36
- Hattie 36
- Lizzie 36
- Ned 36
- Sally A 44
- William 36

WAKEFIELD
- Albert McL 36
- Albert Z 36
- Charley 36
- Edmon S 36

Esco B 36
Kisy 36
Lucy May 36
Lydia E 36
Lydia E M 36
Thomas M 36
Thos Alvin 36
Virginia 36
WALKER
　Eudalia J 36
　John 36
　Mamie 36
　William 36
WALKINGSTICK
　Annie 37
　Bascum 37
　Caroline 37
　Celie 37
　James 36
　Jasper 37
　John 37
　Maggie 37
　Matilda 36
　Mike 37
　Mose 37
　Nation 37
　Owen 37
　Thomas 37
　Walsie 37
WALLACE
　Olly 37
WARD
　Charles J 37
　Clara A 37
　Jennie May 37
WARLICK
　Edna May 37
　Mary Jane 37
WASHINGTON
　Emma 37
　Jesse 37
　Joseph 37
　Key 37
　Lizzie 37

Luzane 37
Ollie Ann 37
Rachel 37
WATERS
　Polly 37, 47
WATTY
　John 37
　Ute 37
WATY
　Lidge 37
　Lizzie 37
　Mary 37
　Nancy 37
　Nute 37
　Royeenih 37
　Steve 37
　Wallie 37
WAYNE
　Sarah John 44
　William J 37
WEBB
　Annie E 37
　Eleanor L 45
　Emily 37
　Ethel 45
　Florence A 45
　James C 37, 45
　John H 37
　Letcher P 37, 45
　Robert A 37
WEBSTER
　Carrie 37
　Jetter 37
　Norma 37
　Rachel A 37
　William L 37
　William R 37
WEINMAN
　Geo B 37
　Jennie E L 37
WELCH
　Adam 37
　Anna E 37
　Arlicke 38

Charlotte ... 37
Clarence ... 38
Corneta ... 37
Davis W ... 37
Eddie ... 37
Eddie R ... 37
Epps ... 37
Eve ... 37
Jackson ... 37
James ... 37
Jane ... 38
Jesse ... 37
John ... 37
John G ... 37
John Goins ... 37
Joseph ... 37
Lee ... 37
Lizzie ... 37
Lloyd R ... 38
Lucinda ... 37
Madeline G ... 37
Mark G ... 45
Mary ... 37
Mary E ... 38
Nannie ... 37, 38
Ned ... 37
Sallie ... 37
Sampson ... 38
Sarah J ... 37
Stacy ... 37
Theodore A ... 38
William H ... 37

WENN
John ... 38
Nancy ... 38

WESLEY
Jinnie ... 38
Judas ... 21, 38

WEST
Faustina E ... 38
Michael ... 38

WESTFIELD
Eliju ... 38
Fannie ... 38

Mollie ... 38
Ralph ... 38
Reese ... 38

WHIPPERWILL
Allen ... 38
Manly W ... 38

WHISENANT
Creola ... 38
Dewey ... 38
Emma ... 38
Lola ... 38
Presley ... 38
Vester ... 38
Vinnie ... 38

WHITAKER
Ada ... 38
David L ... 38
James M ... 38
Jud ... 38
Martha A ... 38
Rutha ... 38
Sarah A ... 38
Stephen D ... 38

WHITE
Anda J ... 38
Bessie E ... 38
Bettie ... 38
Dee ... 38
Dillard ... 38
Walter A ... 38

WHITFIELD
Emma C ... 38

WHITT
Callie ... 38
Gurney ... 38

WHITTEN
Martha ... 5

WIGGINS
Estelle R ... 38
Mildred ... 38

WILD CAT ... 38
Rebecca ... 38

WILDCAT
Alsie ... 38

Index

Lestie 4
Testie 38
Tinola 38
WILKINSON
  Jefferson 38
  Silvester 38
  Wayman 38
  William 38
WILL
  Alice 38
  James 38
  Jane 38
  John 38
  Mooney 38
WILLIAMS
  Arvey 38
  Charley 38
  Claud 38
  Clifford 38
  Daniel M 38
  Fred M 38
  James D M 38
  James Fred 38
  Jennie 45
  Jessie 38
  John H F 38
  Louisa 47
  May 38
  Mollie O 38
  Robert 38
  Wm M 38
WILLIS
  Andrew E 38
  Benny 38
  Early 38
  Mary 38
  Pickens E 38
WILNOTY
  Haggie 39
  Joe 38
  Lanty 39
  Mink 38
  Moses 39
  Ned 39

Nice 39
Sallie 39
Sammon 39
WILSON
  Ancil 39
  Arthur 39
  Edna M 39
  Jefferson 39
  Luther 39
  Margaret N 39
  Mary 39
  Minnie 39
  Monnie 39
  Rosalee 39
  Roscoe 39
  Selma 39
WINDSOR
  Nancy 4
WISHON
  Bertha G 39
  Charity M 39
  Charley M 39
  Gaily O 39
  George 39
  George W 39
  John W 39
  John W, Jr. 39
  McKinley E 39
  Martha E 39
  Pelmina M 39
  Robert C 39
  Thomas J 39
  William T 39
  Willis D 39
WOLF
  Abel 39
  Annie 40
  Jacob 39
  James 39
  Jesse 39
  Joseph 39
  Laura 39
  Nelcena 39
  Owen 40

Index

Rachel 39
WOLFE
  Amanda W 39
  Callie 39
  Charles Hicks 39
  David 39
  Delia Ann 40
  Edison 39
  Eliza Pauline 40
  Elkiny 39
  Emmaneatte 30, 40
  Estella 39
  Francis M. 39
  George L 39
  James 39
  James L 39
  James T 39
  James William 40
  Jasper 39
  Jennie 39
  Jinsey 30, 40
  Job 39
  John 39
  John Albert 39
  John R 39
  Johnnie 39
  Johnson 39
  Joseph 39
  Jowen 39
  Kelly 39
  Kinsey 39
  Linda 39
  Lloyd 30, 40
  Louis David 40
  Louis Henry 40
  Manda Jane 40
  Margaret P 40
  Martha 39
  Mary 40
  Mary E 40
  Mattie 39, 40
  Mollie 30, 40
  Moses 40
  Polly 40

Richard C 39
Sallie 39, 40
Sophronia Iwsabel 40
Susan 40
Thomas 30, 40
Walker 39
Ward 40
William H 39
WOOD
  Hester O 40
  Rachel 40
WRIGHT
  George W 40
  James 40
  Mando 40
  Nellie 40
  Sally 40
  Thomas 40
  Yone 40
WYLY
  Robert M 40
YANAGUSKI
  Lizzie 40
YONCE
  Georgia 45
YOUNCE
  Dasie M 40
  Nancy E 40
  Nancy S 40
YOUNG
  Dora M 45
  John J 45
  Kirby 45
  Mollie 45
YOUNGBIRD
  Dinah 40
  James 40
  John 40
  Rufus 40
  Soggy 40
  Wal-gin-nih 40
  Wesley 40
  Yah-nih 40

YOUNGDEER
- Betsy 40
- Eli 45
- Jacob 45
- Jesse 40
- John 40, 45
- Jonah 45
- Mattie 40
- Moody 40
- Onnie 40
- Steve 40

www.ingramcontent.com/pod-product-compliance
Lightning Source LLC
Chambersburg PA
CBHW020300030426
42336CB00010B/835